D0575909

THE PEOPLE ON SECOND STREET

The People on Second Street

By JENNY MOORE

With an Introduction by Malcolm Boyd

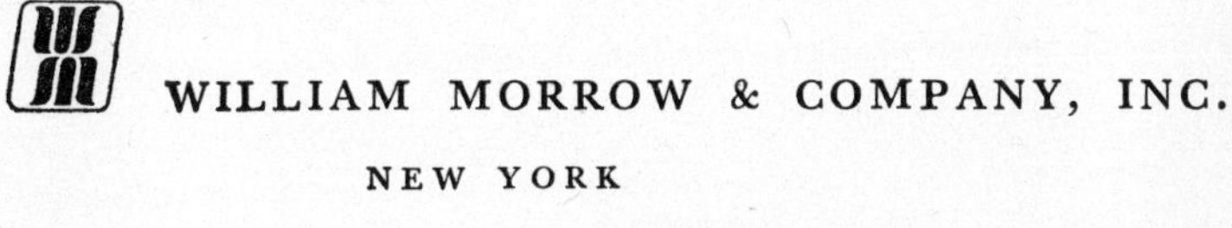

WILLIAM MORROW & COMPANY, INC.

NEW YORK

1968

This is a book about real people in a real situation. However, the names and in some cases the characteristics of people have been changed to protect their privacy.

Published simultaneously in Canada by
George J. McLeod Limited, Toronto.

Printed in the United States of America.

Library of Congress Catalog Card Number 68-21541

To
Paul,
who has led a life worth writing about,
and
to our children:

Honor, who in the midst of confusion was always Honor,
Paul III, who became part of the neighborhood,
Dee, who was born our first summer there,
Rosie, who is the way she is because so many people loved her in her high chair,
George, who says he had his third birthday party in a basement without any windows,
Marian and Danny, who were the last born there, and pretend they remember it,
Susanna and Patience, who have only our memories,
this book is given with love

Acknowledgments

This book would never have been begun without the urging and the encouragement of Kathleen Lobley and Louis Cassels. It could not have been continued without Helen and Dick Dudman whose enthusiasm never failed me, and in whose house I found the necessary privacy for writing. The book would never have been finished without the optimism of Marie Rodell, my agent. Above all, I thank Bill McPherson for his sensitivity, patience and attention as editor, none of which flagged for a moment.

Mason O'Neal, of Jersey City, who spent much of his teens in our house, and who read this book in manuscript, was uniquely helpful. His encouragement rid me of the feeling that it was presumptuous to write this book at all.

J.M.

Contents

Introduction

I am here to "introduce" Jenny Moore as an author. She did once write a single chapter for an excellent book composed by her husband, which I was asked to review at the time. I located the review the other day in some old files, and it contains this paragraph: "A short chapter buried in the book is by the author's wife. It is a classic in its genre. Mrs. Moore should surely be asked, if not compelled, to write a full-length book of her own." Now she has done it.

There is a streak in her manner and writing which sometimes seems cruel. She pushes aside an unbearable weight and gets on with something else; she completes a telephone call and signifies it by simply hanging up; she looks away from a heavy grief in which she has just participated, and smiles because she observes something joyful, innocent, or hilariously funny which attracts her. The semblance of cruelty is, in fact, a mature sort of loving which enables her to function, in grief and joy, in heaviness or lightness.

As the book attests, she refuses to take herself too seriously. This is almost a fetish and can, on occasion, seem an affectation. At the very moment she becomes aware that she has every right to take herself quite seriously, she turns the whole thing around. In such moments, in the book as in life, she has an air of, not dilettantism, but distraction. She reaches out for and finds a lifeline, precisely when she feels self-pity or indulgence coming on. There are incredibly strong connections with other persons' lives here. She focuses in her writing on what she sees clearly, and what she sees is informed by feeling. We are introduced in her book to an extraordinarily zestful and virile cast.

She tells us how she dropped her role of pure observer. She knows she is caught up, as much as anyone else, within the action. There was surely a moment, near the beginning of the story, when she naïvely—or quite pridefully and deliberately, which is more to the point—assumed she could weave in and out of the lines, holding (as to her purse) to the cool of a sympathetic observer. But any illusion that she might be able to pick her moment to be involved, choose her relationships, decide depths and degrees, all this went down the drain.

Here were all the ingredients of Lady Bountiful's chronicle. The clergyman's wife was rich, intelligent, sophisticated, driven, sensitive, pragmatic, keenly aware enough to be the worst snob at court. The story might have become one of those natural disasters: the lady oozing noblesse oblige, and, consumed by restlessness, pillaging alternately within jungles of self and of society. At an incongruously simple-looking turn on a road one day, she chose. No, the way chose her. Then she responded as she did, and walked, for better or for worse, in a particular direction. This lies behind every line, sentence, paragraph.

The book naturally reflects Jenny Moore's lightning moods as well as the intensity of her feelings, which have been so disciplined as to be virtually unrecognizable. And, by careful design, it points beyond herself, and therefore beyond her feelings and moods, to others. This is the book's genius. She shares persons with persons. She spares us the futile and finally vulgar act of moralizing, fending off romantic and sentimental reactions with a sober fury. She does not succumb to ostentatious piety, yet, at the same time, she refuses to engage in a fashionable repudiation of mystery. She will not draw out a reaction by resorting to time-tested and thoroughly accepted methods of literary or religious exploitation. However, with ruthless honesty, she spares us not a whit of passion.

The deep questions which torment and plague us, both the readers of this book and the persons in it, including the author, are almost laughably simple ones. They concern only living and dying. All of us do both of these things.

1-2-3-4-5-6: simple, we say.

4-1-6-3-5-2: complex, paradoxical, irrational; jagged, the jungle, the abyss.

She takes clean, straight, easy lines and somehow holds to their structure with a triumphant clarity, through happenings which show human life sometimes pulled out of any decent shape, as cruelly disfigured as any body lifted from the rack. Her glory is that she never forgets that, in whatever shape, a life is breathing, loving, crying, *being;* as, upon any rack on which it was placed, there is a person created in the image of God, and so meant to love and be loved.

Malcolm Boyd
Washington, D.C.

THE PEOPLE ON SECOND STREET

1 *The Beginning*

That Monday in late June, 1949, was the kind of summer day that makes heels stick to the tar strips of sidewalks. It was a day when a haze around the sun washed away some of the blue of the sky. For my husband Paul and myself, it was moving day. With Kim Myers and Bob Pegram, two priests we had met at seminary, we were on our way to downtown Jersey City and the Episcopal rectory we would all share.

Traffic moved slowly through the Holland Tunnel, and cars seemed smaller as truck followed truck like jogging elephants in a circus parade. Jersey City begins on the other side of the tunnel, and for a while it seemed to consist only of another crowded four-lane highway. From the gutters, little children, mostly Negroes, their arms slack at their sides, peered into car windows when the long metal column stopped for a red light. On the occasional small vacant lot at the edge of the highway, ball playing went on: boys appeared, then scooted into oblivion as if dispersed by the insistent horn blowing, truck drivers' oaths, and policemen's whistles.

Paul turned left on Erie Street and drove slowly, following the moving van. Looking out the window of our station wagon, we saw a Tootsie Roll factory, and smelled the cloying smell that lay heavy in the hot summer air. Near it stood a brown building with an ancient-looking sign, "The Home of Ken-L Ration Dogfood." The next blocks were lined with four-story tenements, brick and brownstone, with an occasional addition of new paint and cinder block. Girls and women clustered on the stoops, a few outstretched arms pushing baby carriages back and forth.

More children with sticks and balls filled the streets. Corners were dotted with teen-age boys surrounding lone girls, or standing in idle male silence. The groups of older boys were either black or white, never mixed. It was the same with the mothers in the doorways. As numerous as the bunches of humanity were the shops, the majority with Polish and Italian names: small groceries, candy stores, laundries and dry-cleaners, the latter with wildly ambitious speed claims emblazoned on their windows.

We rounded a corner directly behind the van, and parked between the towered church and the Victorian rectory at 268 Second Street. As the men began to unload our belongings, the four of us surveyed the scene. A dog lay gasping on the church lawn. The dog was yellow and had a long wispy tail, lank in the grass. Through the tall bars of the fence enclosing the church yard, we saw his flank rise and fall in faint and irregular rhythm. On this short block there was no one about that afternoon. Across the street was the summer-deserted yard of St. Boniface's parochial school. The vague chalk outline of a hopscotch game was visible near the fence. In the corner of the yard, where there was a fraction of air, a little pile of candy wrappers, their crisp gloss long since gone, shifted uneasily against the concrete wall. The show window on the diagonal corner from the rectory was dusty, and behind its smudged glass stood two large rubber plants on the bare counter. "D'Agostino Funeral Parlor" was written in peeling gold script on the plate glass, and beneath it, enclosed in fat-bellied quotation marks, was the phrase "In Business For Years." Directly in front of the door stood an empty rocking chair leaning far backwards from long habit, as if it cradled an invisible body. Overarching the whole area was a vast network of clotheslines grinding on three different stories. The myriads of ropes pulled in the sporadic afternoon breeze, causing their pennants of clothing to flap every which way. Even as we looked, the air became still, and clothes hung shapeless and lonely above the backyards.

Our first act, to which we attached great significance, was to call the ASPCA about the dog. Later, an employee of the Society drove up and carried the now stiffening animal to the back of his truck. The blades of grass where the dog's body had been lay flat at first, but after an hour or so there was no sign of disturbance, only a little bit of froth from his mouth still clinging to one tall green spear, hard to distinguish from the wisps of dandelion that hung nodding in filmy seed.

The rectory was built of brownstone, set back from the structures on either side and about thirty feet from the sidewalk; to its left but closer to the street was a square-towered church of the same stone. A front walk of cement slabs divided the large grass yard that stretched from the back door of the church and the front door of the rectory to the abrupt wall of the adjoining house. The rectory, wedged in the background of this compound, had settled in a slightly off-center stance, and one could imagine someone standing on the gingerbread outline of its roof with a pot of boiling oil à la Charles Addams.

While Paul directed the destinies of the furniture coming off the van and Bob, in his Southern accent, encouraged the grunting moving men up the narrow stairway, Kim engaged in another project. Our yard was separated from the public sidewalk by a metal fence and a wooden, roofed entryway known as a lych-gate. Two benches faced one another under its peaked roof, whose carved Gothic letters invited the passerby to "Enter His Gates With Thanksgiving." On the low gate at the entrance to this structure a crudely painted sign commanded, "Keep Out." Kim couldn't wait. With a hammer borrowed from the moving truck he ripped off the offending sign.

While the symbol-shattering was going on I, seven months pregnant with our third child, stood in my kitchen. The house, dirt and all, was in its own way beautiful. The kitchen had been a parlor in the time of basement kitchens. Its parquet floors were covered with a figured linoleum rug, its walls papered with an even busier red- and cream-colored pattern of gallant little soldiers and cone-shaped trees. A shallow sink on four yellowing legs, of a suitable height for someone four feet tall, stood against the wall. Above it were white wooden cupboards with decals of Dutch girls skipping across the doors. An old apartment-size refrigerator and a still more ancient gas stove, the white enamel pocked with age and use, occupied the opposite wall. In the corner near the door towered the seven-foot church safe, left over, I learned later, from the days when the room had served as a study.

The house had been locked and vacant during most of June. Our immediate predecessors, the Eversons, who had left for a job in the Middle West, had lived in the rectory for about five years. They were childless and had closed off the basement and the third floor. From top to bottom the rectory was airless and thick with dust.

The three second-floor rooms were papered, one with a gay holly print, and two had boarded-up fireplaces and handsome white carved mantels. The light fixtures curving out from the walls were converted gas lamps. The only bathtub was a leggy period piece. Of the same era was a marble washstand whose cracks were filled with old mortar and newer sediment.

After surveying the second floor, I went back downstairs. The movers were finished and the van had left. Paul was just coming in the door, followed by a crew-cut, barrel-chested man with an anchor tattoo partly visible under the sleeve of his T-shirt.

"I heard there was three of you priests," the young man said, laughing nervously. "Everson, the man here before you, told me. Just one of you is married—is that right? Have you got kids already?"

"We have two, but they're in the country until we get settled," Paul answered. Kim and Bob came in at that moment and Paul introduced the man as Steve. We all shook hands.

"I'm the only one on the payroll," Steve said, "and I've got the keys to the church for you. I came and opened the house on my noon hour. I see you got in okay." He laughed again and looked around at the furniture standing in such bulk and disarray. He helped Kim and Bob push a few of the big pieces into corners of the living room.

"I don't think you've got many friends to start with," he said apologetically, as we walked across the hall into the kitchen. "The folks that's here were loyal to Everson, the Church Army worker. They're satisfied with things the way they are—both ends meet you know—and there's a lot of people think you're some fancy Episcopal experiment from New York. There's not many Protestants downtown here anyways, so they stick together. I was raised a Baptist myself, but now Sunday's like any other day for me—I drive a truck seven days a week."

Kim started to tell him we had been sent as a team by the Bishop of Newark to try to put some life into the congregation. "We don't believe the Church should be satisfied with following its members to the suburbs." (Now that we were really here, our theories began to sound hollow and rather grand.)

Steve raked his fingers across the front of his neck and examined the thumbnail thoughtfully. "Sure as heck you're going to have problems, if making changes is what you have in mind. The church is the only thing round here that looks the same after a hundred years. Everything else's different. There's two Negro teen-agers Everson took under his wing, but betcha that stops there. Anyone leaves this section that can, and them that stays haven't much." He finished abruptly and ran his finger along the dust on the top of the safe.

"Maybe you'd better show us how to open that while you're here," said Paul.

"Don't get too excited about what's in it—just a lot of records about how much money everyone used to give." He twirled the brass dial on the safe. The heavy door swung open to reveal shelves of large ledgers. Steve pulled open a drawer and dangled a bunch of antique keys.

"Do we have to learn what all those fit?" Bob asked.

"Everson kept the church locked most of the time. Here's the key to the back door, and then you bolt the front one from the inside. Here's two for the rectory, and some of these rusty ones belong to the church basement—that crypt goes on forever." Before he pushed the safe door shut, he pulled out a large blue leather-bound scrapbook lettered in gold, "My Book of Memories: Grace Church." He leafed through the pages, as we watched quietly. "Didn't paste in a thing after the thirties, I guess."

We thanked him for stopping in and shook hands all around.

"Come by again," said Paul. "We can learn a lot from you."

"I don't get in no discussions with nobody," added Steve. "Enough trouble with my wife—she says I spoil our boy. She wants to move out to Bergen, and I can't afford it. The colored are moving in all around—two blocks away from the church now. My wife says she won't be able to let the kid out by himself before you know it." We followed him out of the kitchen and down the short flight of steps to the sidewalk.

"Well, you won't bother me none—I only work here a few

hours a week, mowing the lawn, cleaning the church. Want me to unlock it before I go?" We walked across the green yard and entered the church. We stood silent. The electric switches clicked loudly. The church lights, enclosed in long rectangular shades hanging on chains from the ceiling, went on up both sides of the nave. Rays of sunlight shone through the tall stained-glass windows and mixed with the artificial light overhead, streaking the pews. The color of the wood was like maple syrup. "I use lemon oil," said Steve, rubbing the back of his hand along the mahogany.

We knelt briefly in different parts of the church. I looked up and saw the phrase "Thou hast overcome the sharpness of death" on the heavy beam across the chancel of the church. I thought of Paul, who had almost died in the war, and tried to guess what he was thinking. His head was bowed, and he knelt a few yards to my left. I wondered if I'd ever get that house settled and my baby born. The sweat ran down the back of my legs.

I got up off my knees impatiently and sat in the pew, looking straight ahead. I remembered as a child thinking that watching another person pray was like peering at someone in the bathroom, so I found myself waiting for a rustle that would tell me the others were off their knees. I assumed that priests didn't befog their prayers with petty details as I did.

It was still light when we went out to find a place to eat. The earliest evening shadows cast uncertain blue streaks on the little clump of irises in the corner of our yard. People were out on the stoops. Some nodded when we said, "Good evening," some stared. A few rushed upstairs and more heads soon appeared at upper story windows. Apparently we were quite a sight in Roman Catholic Jersey City: three black-suited priests and their female companion. I could be identified only as housekeeper or girl friend, pregnant at that.

Second Street was tidy to look at—a couple of small two-family frame houses, a row of four-story brownstones, each one chopped up into eight narrow apartments, or so we gathered from the numbers of heads stuck out windows and of people on doorsteps. The occasional clumps of zinnias next to the doorways were carefully tended. There were patches of jealously guarded grass of that too-pale city-green color, a few morning glory vines with their startling blue flowers journeying up the windows on white string.

The three customers regarded us carefully when we walked into the small counter restaurant. Measuring my large form with a half nervous, half fatherly glance, the proprietor moved out from behind the counter. "The Fathers and the lady would be more comfortable at the table." We introduced ourselves. He grew verbose. "Canon Bryan's church—him that walked his dog and knew everyone in town when I was growing up—it was only the well-to-do went there. I was raised at St. Mary's, across the street from Grace. We all thought your place was closing down. It's not the same here anymore, the coloreds moving in right under your nose. You wake up one morning and there's bottles broke all over the street. Another house gone black, my wife says, when she sees new trash in the gutter."

"We want to do some work with the new people," said Paul—"recreation, summer Bible school, trips to parks."

I could tell from Paul's face that he knew he was sounding like a Boy Scout, but guessed he had decided some comment was better than none. We had to begin somewhere.

"But that's a white church. You're not going to try and mix things up like the Communists, are you?" the proprietor protested. "Now if God had intended a mixture, He'd a done things a lot differently. Have you seen how they live?"

Kim deflected the question by a few comments about housing in general.

"I hear the colored like to be ten to a room," the proprietor went on—"and wait till you hear 'em on Saturday night."

The other customers had gone; we bade him good night. The streets were dark, and the neighbors still talking on the stoops didn't look up. We unlocked the rectory door and sat perched on window sills and cartons. We talked briefly about settling into the house, looking over church records, the first Sunday coming up six days hence; about Steve and the restaurant owner. I think we thought we could change their minds.

The night noises were new: voices below us on the street, the hollow echoes of laughter in doorways until it was cool enough to go to bed, the clotheslines clanking and rattling, and the cats starting their screaming promenade. It took us a long time to get to sleep.

It was just dawn when I climbed from the bed where Paul lay sleeping and walked to the window. I watched the cats losing their footing on the uneven board fences that divided the backyards, leaping from rims of open garbage cans, lifting faces to empty windows. Unnoticed, they would bang angrily with their paws and slither to another sill, finally returning to the clutter of a corner for an angry whirl of sex.

There were night noises in my childhood in the country, where the songs of birds and crickets, even when loud and insistent, had a comfortable rhythm. I thought of the ocean and its primeval comfort, filling my little-girl pillow with a friendly roar.

Morning came. The hot sun flooded through shadeless windows into our room with its pile of unarranged furniture, half unpacked bags, and hastily set up mattress, the headboard standing disconsolate in the corner. A small fan on a table turned back and forth like a silver-helmeted soldier, his head persisting, it seemed that strange morning, in some insane rhythm. Over its hum we could hear someone's voice repeating a phrase. The words were indistinguishable, and we walked to the open window still in nightclothes.

Across the street, in front of D'Agostino's Funeral Parlor,

an elderly man sat in the rocking chair shaking his fist in our direction. "Bunch o' phonies! Where you come from? What you doing, you phony?" he called.

We waved good morning, but his only response was to leave the chair and walk inside. We watched until the rocker had stopped moving.

II *East Side, West Side*

Phonies, the man had shouted. Sometimes we, too, wondered if we were phonies. Our childhoods had been privileged; money was never one of our worries. Paul had been hungry during the war when he was stationed in the Pacific, but that was a different kind of hunger from what we saw in Jersey City. Neither Barnard nor Yale, where we had studied, had brought us face to face with urban poverty. Except for Paul's war experiences and our years at General Seminary on Ninth Avenue and Twenty-first Street in New York, we had led very sheltered lives. Even the seminary experiences on Manhattan's lower West Side seemed distant, brief, and academic that first year in Jersey City.

Paul and I met in the early forties when he was a Marine Corps captain on sick leave and I was a Barnard College student. Paul had come back from Guadalcanal with an almost fatal bullet wound in his chest and three months in a New Zealand hospital behind him. He was decorated with the Navy Cross and the Silver Star for having saved the lives of some of his men under enemy fire. The Marine Corps arranged for him to give speeches at factories to inspire munitions workers, and the New York papers, not yet sated with heroes, wrote stories about him. Sometimes, the reporters asked him what he would do after the war. He answered that he planned to go into the ministry because he had known an Episcopal monk at prep school and had been deeply impressed with his work in the London slums. This made very boring copy apparently; the newspaper stories said instead that Captain Moore, "sitting on the terrace of his parents' large and gracious home in Morristown, New Jersey, reiterated, 'There are no atheists in foxholes.' " What Paul hadn't told the reporters was that the monk had erased the image of a pale Sunday School Jesus with liquid eyes and hairless hands and shown Him as He was—a social radical, the cut of whose profile and toga was irrelevant.

After we met, I continued classes in the daytime, and at night we danced, went to parties. Paul drank too much, and there were times when he told me how dishonest this heroism business seemed, how he really didn't like getting a medal for shooting somebody in the gut.

He was terribly tall, very funny, and exceptionally loving. He took seriously all the events of his life, but himself rather lightly. I was afraid of life when I was twenty-one, having painted for myself an exaggerated picture of a lonely childhood, like one of those tiresome English children who read too much. Paul understood. We fell in love, laughing ridiculously, and found that knowing each other upset the adolescent logic that whatever happens happens to you alone. Everything we talked about seemed afterwards to be part of both our lives.

We were married late in 1944 and lived for eight weeks in what had been the slave quarters of a Virginia plantation while Paul commuted to Staff School in Quantico. The day we arrived our landlord from the "big house" next door had to be summoned because Paul had not only carried me over the threshold but had flung me on the ancient bedstead, which then collapsed with a great creak. Our little frame house was surrounded by plowed fields, red clay roads, seven untended farm cats, and the cacophony of a flock of guinea hens. The house had no furnace but there were wood stoves, and we were too carefree not to be satisfied with green oak to burn.

After a year of teaching young Marines, Paul was declared fit for active duty. There was a short period at a North Carolina camp, a few weeks' leave, and twenty-four hours, which were meant to be three weeks, in San Francisco. I shed the tears common to so many when a box of red carnations, my favorites, came up to the hotel room—we had not known the morning's good-bye would be a final one. Paul was headed back to the Pacific and I was alone and pregnant, for the moment more aware of the former.

After a summer with my parents in Massachusetts, I moved into an apartment on Manhattan's upper East Side, where I waited out the months of pregnancy and the end of the war. My wire that our daughter had been born reached Paul on a troopship on its way back to the West Coast. He cabled his love and congratulations, and when his plane was grounded twice in Texas, another telegram complained about the state's size. Then, finally, he was home.

And how were we to start again? After the war there was an impatience, wild and unforeseen, among people who had been in the Service. For a few months we partied, went to World Government meetings, argued about the use of the atomic bomb. We thought of people we had loved who had been killed, went to their posthumous babies' christenings, complained that General Eisenhower was president of Columbia University, and told our parents in heated tones that the Russians wouldn't overrun the United States, or, for that matter, take over the labor unions.

In the fall of 1946, Paul began his three years at the Episcopal seminary on New York's lower West Side. This drew a variety of family reactions, from that old chestnut, "There's no greater calling," all the way to "He has absolutely *no* choice but the business world with *his* background." Views of our own generation were less conventional: laughter, real and embarrassed, sympathy, and a suspicion that we just might not know what we were doing.

We left East Seventy-third Street, with its monogrammed pram covers, its fancy grocery-store windows filled with alternate rows of thick pink lamb chops and huge grapefruit wrapped in green leaves, and moved to West Twenty-first Street, among banana vendors, Puerto Ricans, and Ninth Avenue drunks, and we did it with a louder, more self-conscious noise than I care to remember.

A majority of the seminarians arrived fresh from college, not war. They seemed satisfied with the Church the way it was, and somewhat unaware of the world. With few exceptions, theological arguments were rooted in the preoccupations of other centuries. We charged into seminary life brimming with enthusiasm for change. There was to be no compromise, and we were sure that with a little luck we could change the world.

It was at about that time that a venerable seminary professor, when introduced to us and our one-year-old daughter, affixed us with an Old Testament glare and said, "Ah, you three can grow up together."

The General Seminary consisted of an entire block of four-story brownstone buildings surrounded by a forbidding wall. It had been founded in 1817 when the surrounding area was farm land, and all the buildings save the main office fronted not on the street but on an acre or so of shrubbery, green grass, and shaded walks, where black-gowned figures strolled to class with arms full of books. The Chapel of the Good Shepherd, also a part of the seminary, could not be reached from the street; its only entrance was from the inside close. Evenings and early mornings, the bell tolled for prayer and students filed in. Student and faculty wives, children, or other occasional visitors were greeted with tepid tolerance; the world cast no shadow on the close.

Outside when students went for coffee and wives pushed babies to the market, they heard the whistles, insistent and triumphant, of ocean liners announcing departure. Ninth Avenue was thick with trucks, shops, and shoppers. On every corner, there were groups of unemployed men. Sometimes one of them would peel off from the little circle, sally jauntily into a dimly lit barroom, and emerge unsteadily a few hours later to rejoin his peers. On the stoops on side streets off the avenues were pathetic piles of furniture—a few chairs, a mattress or two—guarded by little bands of newly arrived Puerto Ricans, virgins to the urban crush. You never knew whether they were waiting to move the furniture in or had just been evicted. How difficult it was, we said, to connect our Episcopal island where men studied love of God and neighbor with the swarming sea around us.

Some of us had heard of Dorothy Day, a Christian radical who ran a hostel for anyone who needed food or shelter and edited *The Catholic Worker,* a monthly penny-sheet that embraced pacifism, anarchism, and voluntary poverty. We asked her to address the student body. She came to the arched gate of the seminary in ill-fitting, shabby clothes (from the hostel's clothing room, she told me later), and we walked to the room where she was to speak. She asked me to pray for her because it made her nervous to make a speech. Afterwards she thanked me for my prayers and said they had helped. I was stunned by her simplicity. I had never met anyone like her. She was a wind from another land—strong, warm, and a little frightening.

She described her younger, Bohemian days. For a while she had been a Communist, but Communism's concern for the poor had not gone far enough. She told of her common-law marriage to an anarchist and of their child, whose birth had brought her such joy and thankfulness that, hardly knowing why, she had joined the Roman Catholic Church, even though her conversion ended her relationship with the child's father. She brought her radical views into the Church and had succeeded in attracting young people to work with her in the Bowery, where she lived among the homeless. There is an old Irish law, she told us, forbidding a man to shut the light from another man's window. Christians should fight for housing, she said, and we must never forget that Christ is always in the face of the poor. When a seminary student asked her how many people in her breadline were converted, she reddened, then quietly said that God cared about their empty stomachs and broken spirits, and not about their baptisms. After her talk we went back to our apartment across the street from the seminary. She refused a drink because she said she couldn't bear the burdens of alcoholics and drink herself.

Summer came, a baby boy was born, and Paul worked in a state mental hospital. The second autumn we gave an afternoon a week to St. Peter's Church, one block from the seminary.

St. Peter's was a typical run-down city church, its reputation hanging by the thread of a prosperous past and the fact that Clement Moore had written "A Visit from St. Nicholas" in its rectory next door. An endowment from earlier days paid for an elderly rector, whose flock on Sunday consisted of a handful of long-time residents of surrounding Chelsea. The church was locked the rest of the time, save for weekly religious instruction for children from the local public school. It was on these afternoons that we grew to know some of those Puerto Ricans we had seen on doorsteps, some Negroes, and children of those white families too poor to move away. By summer the once-a-week contact at St. Peter's had been expanded with the help of General Seminary funds to a full-time recreation program with Paul in charge. There were trips to beaches and parks, baseball; a classmate's wife who was a trained teacher helped us start a nursery school on the seminary grounds. When I was not sitting in the green close with my two small ones, I visited the mothers of the children in the program. Those hours weren't easy. I learned of the chasm between us when I heard a mother say of me as I left her rat-infested flat, "She asks more questions than the relief worker." I had thought I was showing interest.

I learned how difficult it is to be consistent in love when I met Frankie Butler, a little boy who followed me home from St. Peter's and played with my children, who climbed all over the furniture and onto the window sills, who picked up and examined each article in our apartment with the infuriating innocence of the disturbed, who came again and again, and whose life we couldn't begin to change. Sometimes on a summer outing when his hand, electric with need, slipped into mine, I would look at the bubbles of sweat around his mouth and think of my childhood summers—soft gatherings of air and beach to be idled away with sea water drying on my hair.

Frankie's mother greeted us with a brittle, faded smile when we called on her. The smells of cheap wine and stale urine are commonplace to many college students of the sixties, but to us twenty years before, climbing the four flights to Mrs. Butler's door, they were shocking. A young white couple was standing with her in the small kitchen. "Meet Mr. and Mrs. Moore, the Christians," Mrs. Butler said. "This is Connie and Dick, the Communists." They left with a peremptory nod. This was the Alger Hiss year, and Paul and I were startled. We stood for a while, exchanging amenities of the most superficial type with Mrs. Butler. She didn't know how to invite us to sit down, or perhaps didn't want to prolong the visit, and we were too green even to make a stab at putting her at ease. Finally, Frankie bounced up the stairs behind us and tugged at us to leave with him. Mrs. Butler seemed relieved when we said good-bye but thanked us for being friends to her boy. The summer program was almost over, and we didn't see her again. The incident was brief, but it haunted me, and we worried about the summer's loose ends.

We continued to meet our summer friends casually on the streets and weekly at St. Peter's in the fall of Paul's last seminary year. Sometimes I waited for the children I knew at their school, and we would walk together to St. Peter's or take a subway trip to Central Park. But that was too casual.

It was Frankie's behavior that first brought me to the principal's office at P.S. 11. While my own two children played with the paper clips on his desk, Mr. Hochberg skipped from Frankie to his eighth graders. Mr. Hochberg was a homely, Harry Golden hulk of a man, who sat back in his squeaky swivel chair and talked about love. "Frankie is starved, but he needs more than you can give him. I want to talk to you about my girls." He took me to lunch the next day at a diner where we ate huge pickles and sandwiches at one end of a counter of truck drivers and talked above the din of Ninth Avenue traffic. "My girls aren't bad," he kept saying, "but no one cares, takes an interest. Love 'em a little, and I'll have less truants." Before we left the diner, we had arranged to meet Marlene, the girls' leader, on a Ninth Avenue street corner at three o'clock the following day.

His leonine face beaming, hair more disheveled than I had remembered, Mr. Hochberg escorted her to our meeting place as proudly as Lancelot with a newly won Guinevere. He cradled her shoulders with an affectionate arm. "She's a good kid," he said, gave me a shadow of a wink, and lumbered back in the direction of his shabby school. We stood for a moment in the bright afternoon sun. Marlene reached into her shoulder bag and put on another layer of lipstick.

"Let's have a coke," I ventured, hoping the one phrase would somehow manufacture something comfortable for both of us.

"I don't mind—too bright out here," she said and followed me.

The drugstore was crowded, but we found two seats together at the long counter. Each of my overtures was met with abrupt finality: "Mr. Hochberg's okay." "I hate school." "There's too many spicks on my street." She barely touched her coke, and while I drank mine she flattened the straw, wrapper and all, between her thumb and forefinger. "My teacher don't like it when we bring these to class and blow them," she said.

At last I told her about my plan: "You wouldn't want to start a club, would you?"

She brightened and scooped some of the ice out of her drink with a long red fingernail. "Would it be at your church? The kids'd never come—we're all Catholics, and the priest would holler." I told her they could meet at our apartment. Silent again, she sucked all the moisture from the dunking finger.

"Why don't you get the girls together and come next week?" I suggested.

"I don't mind," she said again.

Walking around the corner to our apartment, we were more relaxed, and she chattered on about the girls who'd come. I pointed out our doorway and told her how glad I was that Mr. Hochberg had introduced us. She shrugged. "I'm not a whore like my mother thinks." I made an inane statement to the effect that I knew she wasn't, and turned the key in the front door. She waved from the corner.

I was nervous the day they were to come; I worried that they wouldn't arrive, that our apartment with its high ceilings and old family furniture was too fancy, that they wouldn't say anything, or that they would think me some do-gooder killing them with kindness. My panic began to wear off when they came giggling up the stairs ten strong in tight sweaters and tighter skirts. They shrieked with pleasure over the brick walls and rough beams of our top-floor living room and raced to the window to ogle the students visible in the seminary courtyard across the street. Occasionally they looked to me for comment but for the most part prattled on as if I weren't there.

I met with them throughout the year. One of the girls, only thirteen, died of congenital heart disease. We went en masse to the funeral, the club members dressed in shiny blue jackets we had bought with money raised at dances. The open coffin was in a tiny, ornate Roman Catholic church filled with candles and weeping, black-shawled Italian women. Joanie, with her elfin face and little body that had worn too-small blouses and skirts from the five-and-ten, had suddenly been transformed into a waxen princess in white satin, her lank black hair out of sight behind a misty veil. But the girls were more accustomed to death than I. They wept for Joanie, then forgot her in the immediacy of planning for next Saturday's dance.

Other than their enthusiasm for the neighborhood teenage dances in the seminary gym, previously used only for male basketball, the girls had no relish for organization or projects; their need was to talk incessantly. Most of them were of Italian background living in overcrowded apartments with a mother at work, too many brothers and sisters to care for, and nowhere to go. Perhaps because I was in my twenties at the time, they were able to talk freely about their boy friends and their lives. Sometimes they would tell me of their dreams of getting out of New York to a place where things must be different, but mostly they said they'd always be poor, that men were no good. The warmth and excitement of their talk with one another helped me to forget that they would wind up like their mothers—too many babies, too old too soon.

But for us this was all temporary; Paul was to graduate in

June. We would be leaving the docks and whistles, Marlene and the girls, Mr. Hochberg's patience and love, Mrs. Butler and the Communists, and the streets full of children whose lives were for a while hitched to ours. During this last academic year, we spent long hours with Bob Pegram and Kim Myers, both young members of the seminary faculty. The two men shared our feelings about the neighborhood. There were long evenings when the four of us talked of the new, postwar books we had all read, which told about the Roman Catholic Church in France losing touch with "the man in the street" and of the so-called worker-priests working incognito on docks and in factories to win him back.

Kim's answer to our sense of frustration was soon in coming. Leaning out of his dormitory window one day, he called to us on the walk below, "Why don't we four take a city parish, one of those dead ones? Bob says he'll go, I just talked to him. I'll write the bishops I know and ask about possible places." His biggest ideas and most fruitful ones always seemed this impulsive. Paul and I, standing on the sidewalk, were a little startled as he spoke. We said we would think about it, but I think we had really made up our minds as we stood there. Bob was articulate about his current dissatisfaction, discouraged about his doctorate, enthusiastic in his own, more measured way. Within days the discussion was more about "how" than "if." Kim wrote eight or ten bishops with cities in their jurisdiction. The letter read that two priests and a married seminarian to be graduated the following June would be ready to go to any downtown parish on one man's salary. Paul could support his family on money of his own, and Bob had enough for himself.

Those all-but-deserted stone churches known in American guidebooks as "little jewels," with their tended green lawns, the locked iron fence with dirty children playing in an adjacent gutter—these were what we had in mind when Kim wrote the letters. The responses were cool. A few did not answer at all; a couple of bishops wrote that they thought the idea commendable, but they had nothing to offer. One imagined us "a valiant crowd" but said he couldn't use us at this time. (For comic relief in later years we referred to each other as members of a "valiant crowd.") The only unreserved encouragement came from Benjamin Washburn, Bishop of the Diocese of Newark. He had a place in mind, he wrote, in Jersey City. A layman was then in charge who was a member of the Church Army, originally an English group devoted to work in cities, but he was ready to leave.

After a couple of interviews with the Bishop and a hasty visit by Paul, Kim, and Bob, we decided to move to Grace Church, twelve blocks on the other side of the Holland Tunnel, in what is known (with some feeling, since "the Hill" boasts more affluence) as "lower Jersey City." Once the decision was made, we read up on the area, discovering it was more Roman Catholic than Boston and an industrial area declining in population. We spent a couple of evenings discussing plans; Kim sat and took vague notes on a yellow pad. Yes, we would all live together in the rectory—Bob and Kim on the third floor, and the Moores, including Honor aged three, Paul one, and a dachshund named Chelsea, on the second; the first floor would be common. Kim and Bob would teach one course at the seminary in order to help with finances and to keep in touch with academic life. We would move at the beginning of the summer, leaving our son and daughter at their grandmother's while we settled.

Family and friends asked us with varying degrees of tact how long we would stay in such an area with a family. We told them we didn't know.

III *Lemonade at the Lych-gate*

Our two small children were to be away another week. The house was in such obvious shambles that even the male eye saw it. I was in that cast-a-glazed-eye-at-the-world mood of late pregnancy, when internal focus suffuses any purposeful action with a female vagueness. Excelsior tendrils clung to every surface, and cartons were piled hip high, but I spent my first morning in Jersey City making vichyssoise in an electric blender. Sitting on our dusty doorstep, we exclaimed over the soup.

I wanted masculine support from Paul and our colleagues in dealing with the clutter of the house but didn't know exactly what I wanted anyone to do. Paul would ask me, with what I thought was simulated patience, what needed to be done next, now that he had set up the crib, and I would withdraw into a silent rage after commenting that it seemed obvious that things were not yet *nice.* I have a vivid memory of Bob, wanting to help me with the general mess, wandering around with a dustrag, wiping packing dust off living room lamps while the dirt of years remained in the long-untenanted upstairs bedrooms. Kim, feeling my standards tiresome and bourgeois, hung his clothes on a few hooks and silently disappeared into the lowest regions of the house to investigate the possibilities of basement office space.

The original basement kitchen, an adjoining room, and a bathroom with an eternally temperamental toilet were damp and just as airless as the upstairs. They were filled halfway to the ceiling with teetering towers of periodicals and newspapers from as far back as 1920 and stacks of antique-looking bedpans, their white enamel streaked with cellar dust. Wondering for what good works such a vast number of receptacles might have served, we summoned the Salvation Army. We filled two trucks with the cellar contents, found a desk and a swivel chair that didn't swivel for the basement office, and, brimming with a new sense of accomplishment, turned our energies back to the rest of the house.

Seminary friends came over from New York for the day and valiantly, but unsuccessfully, tried to match screens to windows that had not been opened in years. We put clothes in wallpapered wardrobes that stood in square permanence in each bedroom and used the house's only closets, two tunnel-like areas buried in the eaves of the third floor, for storage.

After three days, the only local people who had been to the house were the employees from the ASPCA and the Salvation Army, and Steve. The neighbors on the block nodded now; we had exchanges with a few of them about the beauty of our church. Quiet and never-changing in the midst of the busy world, they kept saying. Even St. Mary's and St. Boniface's, where they had all grown up, were too noisy; the Thursday busloads of people that came for bingo all the way from Hoboken and Newark were the worst.

By the weekend, Paul, Kim, and Bob, released from a still dirty but functioning house, waded through the parish files and called on some of the people who lived nearby. It became an increasingly familiar refrain that they heard on these visits to Grace Church members: "We want the church to stay the same; everything else is different." "Why, when I grew up, children behaved themselves and the niggers stayed down

South." "You could read about Puerto Ricans in school, instead of hearing them and their crazy language all over the streets and on the subway to Journal Square. (They say they sew beautiful though.)" Some members planned to come to church our first Sunday; others said they would stay home. ("Mr. Everson did a good job—no reason for the Bishop to let him move.") The choir, ten strong, was going to refuse to sing, that was for sure, someone said. There were also stories of personal sadness that they wanted the clergy to share: the death of an only child, the failure to meet the mortgage on the family property ("Now it's a boarding house"), the feud of the two unmarried sisters who lived together and hadn't spoken to each other for ten years.

On Saturday night, after he had cleaned the church and clipped the low hedge of the church's little corner lot, Steve disappeared briefly and came back carrying paper cups of lemon ice for us all.

"I did an extra good job in there tonight for your first Sunday. I don't envy you none—the choir's quit. Never more than thirty to forty show up anyways, but I doubt there'll be more than half that."

"We may look pretty silly in the morning, but we'll do more visiting next week. Numbers aren't everything," said Paul.

Steve shrugged. "Well, I'll catch hell from the wife if I don't get home."

Steve's prediction about numbers proved accurate: twenty people in a church that could seat six hundred. The couple who had lost their son were there, and the gray-haired sisters who didn't speak, sitting apart. The choir, true to its threat, did not sing but sat in a stony-faced row. Paul's mother, who had driven over from Morristown to be with us, sat with me. She whispered to me that the church was beautiful and kindly kept to herself any doubts at what must have seemed a peculiar debut for her son. The tiny congregation was scattered all over the main section of the church, except for the first ten pews, which were empty save for one old lady. Bob and Paul conducted the service, Kim preached and played the organ—softly in order not to drown the tremulous singing efforts of the small and largely female congregation. Kim was diplomatic; he spoke about Mr. Everson's efforts, of how the beginnings of community were here, and said that Christian community meant an exchange of love and the bearing of one another's burdens. Bishop Washburn had sent us to join in this. Christ, he said, knew no boundaries; the whole city was the parish.

The congregation was visibly hot during the sermon but seemed attentive until, as Kim made an especially dramatic gesture, a voice called out from the front of the church, "What the hell's the matter with him?" From where we sat I could identify the speaker as a small lady with a lavender straw hat, sitting almost directly under the high pulpit, fanning herself with a rolled-up section of funny papers. There was some rustling and murmuring from other parts of the church, and a few giggles. Kim cleared his throat, smiled, and wound up his sermon rather abruptly.

Some of the people were warm and friendly as they shook hands afterwards with Paul, Kim, and Bob. They were obviously taken with Kim's confident manner and concern, and flattered by this avalanche of clerical attention. Others were shy and pushed rapidly to the street. Kim's vocal friend in the lavender hat brought up the rear. She introduced herself to me as Mrs. Powell. "You ain't married to all three of them, are you?" she asked and lingered on the sidewalk longer than the others. I assured her I wasn't and introduced her to Paul.

"For the life of me I can't see why there are three priests coming to a down-at-the-heel church like this. Couldn't you get a better job with all your education?" Paul laughed and said we had wanted to come, but she didn't wait for his answer. We watched her as she left, pausing to poke through the iron fence at the purple iris as she rounded the corner.

By one o'clock on Sunday we were alone again in our hot kitchen. We avoided discussion of the number who had come to church and said to each other over and over that we had expected the vocal resentment about the Eversons' leaving, a general coolness, the choir boycott. We reminded ourselves that the French books that had influenced us so much had described similar situations. Wasn't it good not to start with success, we asked ourselves? Numbers aren't everything, after all (just an American pitfall, you know). Better to start from scratch . . . .

That afternoon Mrs. Powell came around again. I don't think any of us will forget that first visit. At seminary you hear about the ever-ringing doorbell in the newly occupied rectory, the steaming apple pie brought to the door by shining-faced choir boys. We hadn't anticipated quite such an idyllic welcome, but all that first week we had thought someone might approach our door. From my kitchen window, I watched her approach the gate, gingerly wipe off one of the seats with the black bag she carried, hook her cane over the arm of the bench, and sit down. At first she didn't look my way. I thought I was mistaken, that it wasn't Mrs. Powell at all, and that the lavender hat was just a coincidence. It was just someone pausing briefly, and if I went out to say hello, she'd leave. She sat very straight, her knees apart, her stockings bunched and wrinkled around her legs, and her hand gripping her cane as though it were a weapon. I began to notice hasty glances in my direction. My week-long fear that no one would ever speak to us began to melt, and I shouted upstairs, "I think that lady I met after church has come to see us!"

Kim took one look from his window and raced out in shirt sleeves to welcome our visitor. "Hurry up with some lemonade. It's important that she feel she belongs," he instructed me on his way out the door in one of his usual mixtures of commonplace and cosmic.

Paul and Bob were both working in the newly created basement office. They heard the dialogue, stopped what they were doing—thinking it a crucial pastoral moment as well—and walked out to greet her. I hurriedly tumbled some cubes into a pitcher, unaware that ice cream had melted into the ice section of the freezer, and with lemonade and glasses on a tray careened out to join the group. Paul turned to take the tray from my hands. With horror I watched it tilt, slip, and crash to the ground. Lemonade, ice cubes, clots of vanilla ice cream showered on our visitor. Startled, she jumped to her feet and grabbed her cane. She wiped the liquid from the wisps of her still brown hair, pulled her round straw hat off her head, shook it, and put it back on again. "Feel a damn sight cooler," she said, brushing off my apologies the way she had dealt with the shower bath.

In chorus we urged her to come in the house, but she insisted on staying where she was.

"You shouldn't have to put up with a whole lot of people in and out of your house. Lots of members never been asked in that house—just ain't never been, that's all." We decided it was not the time to press the invitation, so instead we sat on the two narrow lych-gate benches, Kim and Bob on one side, Paul, Mrs. Powell and I, a little crowded and bolt upright, facing them. She told us she was one of the office cleaners at City Hall.

"Bunch of chiselers down there. Republican all my life, but they forgot to ask me how I voted and I got the job. Never worked till I was widowed."

She had to get up at four, she said, to have the place cleaned by nine, but then she had the rest of the day off and Sundays as well. It was hot in her little flat, but she had the fan and radio to keep her company and the church on Sundays. I looked down at the scrawny little legs beside me and imagined her on her knees scrubbing the floors. "Them spitoons's hell to shine," she said. She rapped on the concrete with the end of her cane.

"What's happening to me is what's happening to me, but what the devil is the likes of you doing at a church like this? Everyone who can, leaves," she said. "I'm a Republican and a Protestant, so no one in this town ever paid *me* off or I'd be gone, too. The rest of the Episcopals go to those big churches out in the suburbs." Paul tried to tell her that other people moved in when those people left, that this church wasn't a club, that everyone would be welcome at Grace Church. Mrs. Powell remained unimpressed.

"Lot of rubbish," she snorted and went on to describe the new church her niece went to in Englewood. "All the members from the same section of town, and they raised enough money in one year to build a new parish hall. It even has carpets in the halls."

IV *Anyone Could Tell You*

No matter what we did, the fact remained that the dying church was regarded as a bastion against the future by people deeply attached to the neighborhood yet haunted by the fact that the world had passed them by. Their section of Jersey City had once been fashionable, and the current residents clung to the verbal tradition about those greener days with aboriginal tenacity. It was always "how things used to be." Generations told generations. Anyone could tell you.

Grandparents of the querulous worshippers we knew had grasped the wrought-iron railings of their elegant brownstones, driven in carriages to their beautiful Grace Church. There they had nodded to their neighbors in the soft buzz of Sunday greeting, smoothing skirts and coattails on the new brocade cushions of the mahogany pews. Years later, when the ironwork on the same houses had begun to rust, closed curtains in the top-floor windows sealed off the rooms of sons seeking fortunes elsewhere. Those descendants that stayed in Jersey City walked to church to sing the same hymns as their silken-gowned grandmothers, in emptier pews. They grew old behind shutters; or a modest sign above the doorbell advertised "Rooms for Rent"; or they sold their houses to be made into apartments, keeping a few rooms for themselves. Some, like Mrs. Raymond, were still there in 1949.

Mrs. Raymond of First Street was baptized at Grace Church as her mother had been before her. Her arthritis kept her housebound (although Mrs. Powell doubted its seriousness—"She can tiptoe backwards in the dark, I wager, but she gets herself more attention this way").

Except in cold weather, the first-floor window of Mrs. Raymond's flat was always open. She sat sideways with an elbow on the sill, her starched flowered cotton dress the background for a huge yellow cat cradled in the crook of her arm. Preening with self-love, a distant relative of those cats that yowled in their world of nights and ash cans, Mrs. Raymond's pet looked askance at the world and possessively at his mistress. From her vantage point at the window, Mrs. Raymond could see our house and narrow backyard. We met her in those first summer days; there was a card in the file that said she gave a quarter a week to the church. Mrs. Powell pointed her out from our kitchen: "Used to be around the church all the time till she come down with these attacks—son's heavy drinking done it, if you ask me. Made her so nervous she never left home, and her bones froze that way."

The first day I visited her, she pushed the cat off her lap and rolled her chair across the glossy kitchen linoleum to open the door for me. "I didn't have a caller save my daughter and the milkman in the three months before the fathers started coming. Now, rest yourself on one of my wooden chairs." She searched my face with her eyes, shockingly dark in the fish-bone whiteness of her indoor skin. "Canon Bryan was at the church when Mildred and Jerome were growing; then we had the whole house. We never missed a Sunday, even when my husband died. We took in boarders, then Mildred married and moved out to one of the Oranges. The Sunday School was only a handful, and my fingers were stiff even then. Jerome never took much interest in religion once he was raised—now it's him and me just. It's been seven years since I been out of the house.

"But even so, the church means everything to me. Me and the cat here can see the tower perfect in the sky. At night when Jerome carries me into bed, I can still see it, but the church shape looks different lying down. Maybe you know all this; your husband gave me communion last week and we talked. A lifeline, that's what I told him."

I was a little startled, embarrassed that she was able to tell me something that was so close to her, and yet I was touched at the same time. I bent over to pet the cat, who had curled himself halfway around my ankle. Only a minute passed, but I was aware that she was talking again and I wasn't paying attention. My comments, when she paused, were acknowledged by a nod.

"Jerome's a good boy," she said. "He never missed a day of work in thirty years. Never married either. He helps me to bed, to the toilet even, cooks and irons for me—says he watched me work for so many years he didn't hardly need to learn. He's home by four o'clock—works for the railroads cleaning coaches." She paused and glanced at the clock on the refrigerator. "Mildred gave me one of them Big Bens. It ticks so loud it almost talks."

Before I left, there was a grating of the key in the lock, halting, finally clicking. Jerome walked in unsteadily; his voice was thick. "Turned it the wrong way first off." He examined the key in the palm of his trembling hand, holding it close to his eyes.

"Hang it up on the hook, Jerome, before you lose it. Meet our new neighbor from the church." Jerome, with the elaborate motions of alcoholic indirection, finally found the end of the hook, and rubbed both hands on the side of his work pants.

"Pleased to meet you. Mother looks to find you people through the windows of your house, she tells me." He bent to kiss her, his cheek pressing hard against the frail yellowing halo of her old-lady hair. His kiss resounded in the air.

Mrs. Raymond lifted her hand with difficulty from the arm of the wheelchair, and her lumpy fingers stroked his arm.

"Aim better next time, Jerome."

I rose to go. Mrs. Raymond grasped my hand. "Come back, come back—and when your children's home, bring them. I see the grandchildren so seldom—too far, Mildred says."

Jerome held onto the back of his mother's chair, rocking on the balls of his feet. "What was that hymn I sang as a boy, Mother?" He gave me a big wink over her head. "Fight the fight, maintain the strife, strengthened with the bread of life."

She hummed unevenly along with him, and swayed a little in the wheelchair. "Three generations in the choir, can you beat that? Now, don't forget to come back."

I felt chastened as I closed the green door behind me and Jerome's raucous voice embarked on another hymn. I had left the rectory believing that I was going to give Mrs. Raymond a lift with bright banter. Instead, she had outtalked me, almost excluding me from conversation.

Mrs. Powell was sitting in our kitchen when I returned. She had slipped firmly into our lives within a week after the lemonade shower, stopping by regularly on her way home from work in the morning or sitting with us at suppertime. "Mrs. Marlowe wants you folks over for supper," she said. "I told her your own kids weren't coming home until tomorrow so you was free to go. She's going to have the other fathers next week. Fancy that—family silver and all. Now why do you think she had to run through the damn menu with me? She thinks she's better than the whole bunch of us."

There was no question about our accepting Mrs. Marlowe's invitation. It was the first such gesture, and from what we had heard, she had been the most vocal supporter of the departed Mr. Everson and his wife. Paul remembered her excusing herself with the merest of greetings the first Sunday.

She lived a block from us in a yellow stucco two-family house, newer and tidier than the rest. There was no stoop, and its front door, unlike that of its neighbors, was set back a few feet from the sidewalk. A little row of privet hedge outlined the front walk; a red rosebush splashed color on the stucco and covered the corner drainpipe with its glossy leaves. The house was unlike the tenements with their wide-open entryways; there was no way of getting in the building without ringing. When we arrived, Mrs. Marlowe called down from her window that she would press the buzzer. She appeared nervous when she greeted us and straightened the vase of artificial flowers on the table in the front hall.

"My boy, Leo, can't stand a bare foyer," she said, the little scratchy lines widening around her mouth but never quite becoming a smile. She was quite lovely, with soft graying hair held in a loose bun and young eyes so frail and blue they drew attention away from the anxious lines around them.

"It's been a while since I entertained," she apologized. "I almost forgot to ask you to sit down." We followed her into the carpeted living room. A curved sofa, upholstered with worn velveteen, dominated one side of the room. Two matching armchairs almost facing each other made a little triangle with a small table. Another low table, almost completely covered with an oversized crocheted doily, stood in front of the sofa. Nothing seemed to be out of place.

"My friends have all moved, so my only socializing is at the store. I work at the jewelers on the Square—watch out for the broken spring," she told Paul. "I brought that chair from my mother's house when she passed away, and it's never been fixed. I had Leo to raise and I was already a widow."

"You were so nice to ask us over," I ventured.

"Well, I had to explain to Father—I was close to Mr. Everson, and he knew Leo's problem. I just can't understand the Bishop letting Mr. Everson go, after the years he put in here. He was more our kind than you people from New York—

grew up in Hoboken just twelve blocks from here—I know the section."

"We met Mr. Everson. I think he had planned to leave . . . ."

"Well, I don't bear you no grudge," Mrs. Marlowe interrupted. "The church is always welcome in my house—but I won't be able to stay. My house is for sale. The sign goes up this week." She plumped pillows on the vacant chair as she spoke, a word here and there losing itself, it seemed, in the shadows of the shuttered room. I had to strain to hear her. She held her slender hand to the crack between the shutters, and a shaft of evening light caught the gold of her wedding ring. "I forget how long summer days are. Now, Father, you must pour the wine or Leo will never forgive me. Wine's a job for men, he tells me." She pointed to the low table and a small tray painted with pink cabbage-like flowers. On it stood three glasses, their clear amber stems fading to a milky rim. Paul half filled them from a matching decanter. "This set reminds Leo of jewels," said Mrs. Marlowe, holding up her glass. The heavy wine lay like honey on my tongue.

"It hits the spot," I lied.

Mrs. Marlowe sat on the chair near Paul, holding her glass with both hands. Paul leaned forward. "Tell us about Leo. I haven't had a chance to speak to him. Was he with you Sunday?"

"Leo used to help Mr. Everson with the service some, behind the scenes, you know, where he wouldn't be asked a lot of questions. Sunday he was too shy." She twisted the stem of the glass. "Leo, my only son, is waiting for an annulment of his marriage to Princess—that was her given name. I don't understand. I just loved that girl—and my neighbors —they're all Roman Catholic—keep asking me where she's gone."

She showed us the tinted photograph of Princess that hung behind the velvet sofa. We agreed it was hard to see anything in the delicate brow and soft eyes that would explain why she had left Leo. "She *was* young," Mrs. Marlowe added, "but just as precious to me as Leo is. There was some question about consummating the marriage, as I understand it from the lawyer." She turned to the photograph again. "Why, Leo couldn't keep his eyes off her at the wedding–it was in the church. Since he was a little boy, he'd told me how he wanted to fall in love with a brunette. And with that dark hair, you'd think it would've been perfect." Paul told her he would telephone the lawyer, if that would help, to see whether the proceedings could be hastened.

She brightened a little. "Well, maybe you have influence. Mr. Everson was in touch with him a couple of times, and he said the Church had no business getting into legal matters. I sometimes wonder what kind of lawyer he is, it's been so long now."

"Well, it can't hurt for me to call him–and I really feel it's my job and the Church's," Paul said. I wondered if she believed him.

"I'll appreciate it," said Mrs. Marlowe. "Enough of my troubles; you must be hungry." She walked to the little dining alcove off the living room. I swallowed the rest of my wine.

"Please be generous with yourself. The potato salad's Princess's recipe. I fixed it last night, but all I had time for today was cold cuts. I stopped at the store on my way home." She stood in the doorway. There was a heavy brass chandelier over the round table, with pale beaded shades on the bulbs. The table, with its cream-colored lace cloth, was covered with dishes–two small silver containers of candies, a woven basket of bread, and at one end bologna, salami, and ham arranged on a white platter, each pink circumference barely touching the next.

"It looks beautiful," I lied again.

"Grace, Father?" We bowed our heads. Paul asked a blessing.

"I said it was enough of my troubles, but I did want to explain why I won't be coming back to church—too many questions about Leo. I'll say my prayers though. Be generous with yourself, do, please." She passed the pickles again.

"What was it like when you grew up here?" I asked.

"So different—they cleaned the streets, and Mayor Hague built that beautiful new hospital. The maternity wing is named for his mother. That's where Leo was born. It seems like yesterday, and here he is twenty-five. But it's not as clean as it used to be—" she lowered her voice—"all colored help. I'm not interested in politics myself, but I was raised a Democrat." She ran her fingers over the tablecloth.

"I'm talking too much. My friends at work think Leo's still married, living with Princess in the front room like they did at first, so I really have no one who knows."

"Here I am, Mother. You're so busy talking I knew I could surprise you." Leo stood with his thin frame almost clinging to the alcove doorway.

"I suppose you're talking about my problems; Mother always takes them too seriously." He shook hands with us both. "I thought of the ministry myself when I was an acolyte."

"Leo served the altar till he was through high school. They gave him some kind of medal," his mother interrupted.

"I'm what you people call a backslider, but I liked the church as a kid—I'll join you for dessert, Mother."

We ate our way through mounds of ice cream frozen in shallow dishes of the same amber glass. Mrs. Marlowe was quiet now.

Paul turned to Leo. "We're trying to persuade your mother to stick with it at the church, at least until she moves. Can you help us?"

"Can't do a thing with her—she's run my life since I was born." He pushed his chair back from the table. "That's your job, but I don't know how far you'll get." He patted his mother's shoulder. "She's going to have to spring me when she leaves this house. I've got rooms over the curio shop I run in New York. That's where the bread basket came from. We import."

We excused ourselves soon after Leo left. I had said approximately three sentences in two hours, Paul little more. But Mrs. Marlowe grabbed my hands warmly as we thanked her. "It helps to talk."

Paul and I walked home somewhat confused. We had been generously entertained by a mild, hard-working woman not far from retirement but light-years away from her only son, and hurt by the Church because Mr. Everson, who had befriended her, had been removed from his job. There was no deep grief to assuage, no anger to meet, no sharp fears to dispel—just her problems to hear, their vexing edges dulled by gentility. Seminary had not prepared us for these undefined situations.

We never saw Leo again and saw Mrs. Marlowe only infrequently. Her house was sold quickly, to a speculator who put in a few partitions and rented the building as individual furnished rooms. Mrs. Marlowe was relieved when Paul was able to tell her that Leo's annulment was all set. Princess had signed it, of course, and Leo would shortly. There'd be no problem with the judge; the grounds were apparently sufficient.

Mrs. Marlowe herself moved to the other end of town, but the church there was not at all what she expected—"Stuck-up," she said when she came back one Sunday—so she had given up church entirely, except, of course, for Christmas and Easter. "I couldn't live with myself if I didn't come those two days."

V *Lucille, Howdy, and the Gypsies*

"You can hear Canon Bryan's ghost in the rectory late at night clanking his keys, or if you stick your head out real early, he's on the street with his dang dog. And it ain't only people on this block's seen him since he died, wearing one of them long black skirts these fathers wear," Mrs. Powell declared. Canon Bryan, who preceded Mr. Everson, had presided over the last traces of wealth in the parish, and had witnessed the exodus to the suburbs of many of its members. He had been in high favor with Frank Hague, Jersey City's world-famous political boss, who reigned from 1917 until 1947.

It was the end of our second week. Mrs. Powell and I were sitting outside watching Honor, almost four, playing in the yard. Her mind was not geared to Mrs. Powell's comments, but she didn't miss the ghost details. "That lady says he has keys to the doors, but he's dead," reported Honor at supper. Years later she told me she used to lie awake worrying that Canon Bryan would emerge from a shadowy corner of her room. The children slept in a second-floor bedroom adjoining ours; next to its little boarded-up fireplace was a narrow, deep closet obviously intended for brooms and mops. Honor had assumed, from the vantage point of her bed, that its recesses were the perfect ghost hideaway.

The children, as the days progressed, learned to sleep through the cat noises at night and to disregard Mrs. Powell's eerie yarns. They had sidewalk tricycle races and played with Lucille's children in front of our gate.

Lucille lived next door to us and was my first acquaintance on the block. Her swarthy, taciturn husband, Tony, worked nights and spent the days sleeping. He would emerge to drink beer or orange soda on the stoop, thoughtfully fingering his sleeveless undershirt as he watched his three equally swarthy little boys trundle about on dusty tricycles. Lucille sat endlessly on the same stoop. When Tony joined her in the late afternoon, she would greet him with a sideways nod, and they would exchange a few monosyllables. She was almost always silent, except for overanxious comments directed at her children, who, mosquito-like, would dart in mysterious formation around garbage cans and telephone poles. Occasionally she would produce some coins, and the oldest child would clatter off, legs spinning with the rusty tricycle spokes, hurrying to the corner for ice cream cones, which would soon be dribbling on three delighted chins. Their middle-aged grandmother, arms folded on the sill, eyed the street's activities from an upper-story window, as though it were the bridge of a destroyer.

Lucille was little more than a girl. Her blond hair hung curled and very long; heavy rouge and lipstick accentuated her air of discontent. She looked like a combination of a yellow-haired doll in a Christmas show window and Mildred, from *Of Human Bondage*. Sometimes we would meet up at the corner, where there were a couple of public benches on a little triangle of grass. We would exchange pleasantries about the weather and the children, but we were both ill at ease in the early days. She seemed never to take her eyes off her little boys. Perhaps because she was the first young mother I knew in Jersey City, Lucille haunted me. She was fettered by her children and their runny noses, and by thoughts she already knew were only dreams.

Unless her mother came down from her upstairs perch to baby-sit, Lucille was always surrounded by children. Ours were asleep by seven-thirty, but hers would be scooting around the stoops way into the night until the last street voice was silent. The family slept late in the morning and rose when we would be thinking of lunch.

The first time Lucille came furtively into our yard in search of a missing tricycle was as much of a milestone as Mrs. Powell's first visit. Our front yard, by unspoken agreement of our neighbors, had appeared to be forbidden territory. The offensive "Keep Out" sign was gone, but Lucille pushed the gate open gingerly, as though it were electrified. Dragging the reluctant hand of the little boy behind her, she made her way up the walk with anxious glances toward the street. I waved from the kitchen window. "They can play here anytime," I called.

"His father'll whack him for this," she answered, seizing the tricycle, "and he'll holler at me for coming through the gate." She pushed the uncomprehending culprit back to the sidewalk.

Strangely, as though some initiation rite had been observed, this proved a beginning, and often Lucille would join Mrs. Powell's afternoon vigil on our side of the iron fence.

Around the corner from the church was a candy store where people also bought newspapers, delicatessen food, soda, and, on hot summer evenings, lemon ice in shallow, pleated paper cups. The store's proprietor was an impassive man with white hands and a tall, A-shaped body invariably encased in baggy brown trousers and a short-sleeved nylon shirt. He had few reactions: a reluctant smile for a baby, a swift closing of the store if there were any arguments among the customers. Although he was known as Howdy, he was anything but garrulous; his conversation was limited to a sullen, almost inaudible "Hi," delivered with the head lowered. There were no good-byes.

Mrs. Powell felt a formal introduction was necessary, although I was already one of Howdy's customers. Following her through the door one day with Honor and Pip, I caught sight of Howdy half hidden by a teetering pyramid of Baby Ruth bars. He disappeared into one of those mysterious little areas that seem to be in the back of every candy store. It was obvious he had heard or seen us. We waited, alone in the room, the children pressing their noses against the dusty glass cases full of cylinders of sweets, cold cuts, cheese, and open-topped jars with rounded ends of pickles emerging from the greenish brine like the humps of mysterious monsters. The candy store smell, so thick you felt you were tasting it, hung around us in the still afternoon heat. Howdy emerged from the back, pushing aside the mottled-gray plastic curtain that hung on rings over the doorway.

"Wake up, Sleeping Beauty," snapped Mrs. Powell, "you have some customers." Still silent, he burrowed his hand into the freezer for the children's popsicles and accepted the money. "These here are some of the new folks from the church around the corner," continued Mrs. Powell. Howdy grunted in answer to my hello. The introduction was over. We walked back to the rectory.

Toward the middle of July a friend of Bob's gave us a television set, a novelty in 1949. We set it up in the parish hall that adjoined the church and opened its doors to passersby each evening. That first summer Howdy became a TV devotee. He would leave the store in his younger brother's care and come and stand in the back of our hall with whatever priest was in charge. As news of the television set traveled, our audience increased rapidly to thirty or forty people. We seated them on the folding wooden chairs we found stored in the parish hall kitchen. They had been stacked against the tall, slatted doors of cupboards filled with shelf after shelf of heavy tan china marked with a church emblem, legacies of bygone banquets. Lucille, her husband, her mother, and the little boys often drifted in. Mrs. Powell came periodically, loudly commenting on the narrative or some Western movie. Other faithfuls included a couple of widows of Mrs. Powell's vintage, who had "known this lovely old church since we were girls." Sometimes people walking to the subway or to larger stores on Newark Avenue, four blocks farther on, stopped in. "We used to be asked over here regular, to a bridge or some other card party. Canon Bryan knew us all. Everything's changed now." Often these were chatty evenings, the general conversation punctuated by Mrs. Powell's observations, kids telling her to be quiet, and by the noise of others moving their chairs closer to the screen.

"There won't be no more radio programs before you know it," Mrs. Powell declared after one of her first television experiences. It seemed to irritate her that she drew a buzz of agreement from her cronies, and she would rap her cane on the floor as if to signal she was ready either for silence or for a new topic.

These evenings were the only times Howdy spoke more than a word or two, and his sociological asides were the source of much of our information: the pinch that came with the lifting of rent controls ("Twenty-five dollars a week for a stinkin' hole that used to be seven bucks, with cat shit all over the stairs"), irritation that the neighborhood was changing ("They're still on the other side of Newark, but those niggers'll take over, you wait and see"). These and other nuggets popped out of the side of Howdy's scarcely moving mouth, with long pauses in between when he would turn his attention back to the TV.

Everyone remembered what used to be. The streets used

to be cleaner; there weren't bunches of grown-up boys huddled, hands in pockets, on street corners; houses were repaired.

"When my husband was alive . . ." was Mrs. Powell's introduction to her version of nostalgia. "He ran his own carpeting business, at least till the Depression. We owned our own home on Erie Street." Sometimes in the midst of one of her stories the television program might catch her interest and she would pause, continuing her story minutes later, assuming everyone around her could pick up the narrative thread she held so firmly. "It was two floors, and just as nice as some of the homes those City Hall folk got on the Hill. Now a bunch of gypsies live in it, and God-knows-what goes on upstairs."

Soon I became acquainted with the gypsies, a term I had relegated to tambourines, Halloween, and *The Blue Fairy Book* or other childhood literary fantasies. Early one evening toward the end of July, I heard a babble of voices in some unrecognizable tongue float up from the yard. My children crowded with me at the window, pointing with disbelief, as if they were seeing mermaids flipping up the path on their tails. Peering over the children's heads, I watched the clutch of storybook characters dressed in a clash of wild pinks and orange. We went down and I opened the door for a stout, immediately aggressive middle-aged woman with oily black hair coiled around her head and huge gold hoop earrings barely clearing the heavy moles at the curve of her neck. She elbowed her way in the door, past me and the children. Behind her were two younger women, heavily made up, with bright-colored taffeta skirts ruffled to the floor and metal bracelets that covered their arms almost to the elbows.

"We are gypsies. These are my girls—and I am Mamma." The girls responded with what looked to me like flamenco hip-shaking. Mamma wore the same white flounced blouse as her daughters, but her skirt was above her ankles and of a simpler stuff. The transparent blouses were becoming to the thin, olive-brown arms and throats of the two girls but repulsive on Mamma, whose mottled arms and heavy-hanging breasts were ill-concealed by pink underwear. Mamma launched into a torrent of words increasingly hard to identify as English, though the word "money" occurred over and over again. Honor and Pip retreated to the stairs, where they watched in silent fascination. Something told me not to move from the front hall or the visitors might never leave. The monologue hurtled on. "You pretty lady, you get new baby." The bangled hand patted my stomach.

"You no watch TV? We can watch? Where is eet?" Without waiting for an answer, she patted my stomach again. "You feed your lovely children. I have no money for the food." Not sure she could absorb anything I said, I turned to the daughters, who were batting their bland, expressionless black eyes at me over Mamma's shoulder.

"We have TV in the parish hall. The door is right next to Howdy's," I told them.

"Howdy no give me credit," she almost screamed at my mention of the candy store. "My Baby starve!" I hadn't seen "Baby" hidden as he was by the semidarkness and Mamma's bulk. Baby, whose real name Mamma explained was Sam, stepped forth from the doorway at her wail. He was at least eleven, pink-cheeked, shining of eye, and appealing. I remember thinking at the time that Sam was a most unlikely gypsy name. He must stem, I mused, from a tortured romantic dance near a flickering campfire in the vague direction of Hungary. Nevertheless, here was Sam, and I had to deal with him. His English was fluent. He explained that they hadn't lived here long and that he had no father. At the word "father," Mamma groaned noisily, and feeling apparently that Sam was not convincing enough, she told him to shut up and shifted to a series of unintelligible sounds. While she and the girls conferred busily among themselves, Sam spoke up again to volunteer that this was gypsy language.

Any initial sense of romance I had had at meeting the gypsies had flown. We had been standing in the hall for what seemed like hours. Mamma had not yet listened to my answer to her original question about the television. She seemed oblivious to my presence as she stood in a verbal huddle with her daughters. What would become my unassailable exit line, "I've got to put the children to bed," broke up our interview. Before I went upstairs, Mamma gave my stomach a final poke, "Eet's a girl." Then she sailed off, mumbling dissatisfaction, docilely followed by Sam and the girls.

I was ashamed that she revolted me so. I knew that we could not choose the strangers who came to our door any more than we could select our neighbors, and I had believed that my good intentions would tide me over situations like this. It was not that easy, I discovered the day that Mamma first descended on me.

The gypsies never came to the television evenings, but for a week or so they came to our door almost daily, each time the whole family, each time a new story, with rosy-cheeked Sam running verbal interference for Mamma's attack—"She means we didn't have any breakfast."

One of their visits marked the only time any of us ever saw Bob angry during the years we were together. He was standing with them in the front hall, Southern accent more Southern, his voice suddenly loud. We were all secretly jubilant that his patience was finally defeated. Mamma and the girls were bombarding him with elaborate stories of their various deprivations: poor little Sam needed surgery, the rent was due, and on and on.

"I'm not at all sure you are telling me the truth," we heard Bob say. Mamma followed with another spout of words, interrupted by Bob's exasperated "Well, *you've* got to listen to *me.*"

I crept down from upstairs to peek. Mamma and the girls were gliding in an ever-tightening circle around Bob, whose balding head was pinker than usual; Mamma was still talking. Sam stood embarrassed and silent near the door.

"If you won't listen, you've got to go." In desperation, Bob managed to break out of the dance routine they were carrying on around him and literally pushed them out the door.

According to Howdy, Mamma always found enough cash to buy supplies from him. We concluded that we would never get the real story from Mamma, and Bob decided to talk to a few of the shopkeepers in the gypsies' neighborhood.

I had been spending almost all my time in the house or on the immediate block, so I made up my mind to take the children and accompany Bob on his fact-finding mission. My third baby was due soon. I was self-conscious about venturing abroad, especially since Honor had that week told a Roman Catholic neighbor that her father was a priest and her mother a cook. Nevertheless, out we went, Bob in black suit and clerical collar, and I, pushing one child in a stroller and holding the other by the hand. We walked the six or seven blocks down to Mamma's place. Signs of decay were all around: too many cats sleeping in display windows, crumbling curbs, trash and dirt caked in the gutters. Almost every block had a one-room grocery with Italian and Polish specialties: pasta of every shape, sausage of every hue and convolution, unwrapped and reposing on squares of waxed paper in the shop window. At the various shops Bob inquired about the gypsies. His round collar gave him carte blanche in Jersey City, even in the company of a pregnant female. The proprietors didn't hesitate to talk about the gypsies, and they all told Bob much the same story: Mamma was an incurable liar, the girls were rapidly hardening in the same mold, and they all felt sorry for "the kid, the one the old lady calls Baby." None of them would give Mamma any more credit. "She don't need no miraculous medal to find a five-dollar bill—it's hid in her underwear" was Howdy's summary.

Before we went home, we walked by Mamma's quarters, a storefront draped with an opaque, billowing material. While we were watching, the cloth parted in the center like a stage curtain and one of the girls' heads appeared, tilted demurely, the pink material held tightly around her face like Lawrence of Arabia's battle headdress. She cast sidelong, beckoning glances at the men on the street, and after a few moments the desired contact was apparently made and she discreetly withdrew, the curtain falling straight and full. As an impressionable twelve-year-old, I had been told that I would be carried off into white slavery if I went to the movies alone in Gloucester, Massachusetts—kidnapped right out of my leatherette seat in the Rialto Theatre. And here I was, gaping at a brothel of sorts with my two children in either hand.

Sam emerged from the doorway before we left, his little-boy chest showing through the buttonless shirt that Mamma had cut down for him from one of her tawny-orange garments. He walked back to the house with us and played ball with Honor and Pip in the front yard while I fixed supper.

VI *"Move Along, Nigger Boy"*

Horatio raised his hand, and the loose sleeve of his shirt fell back from his small arm.

"Father, Dennis has to go to the toilet something awful," he said in a clear childish voice.

" 'And the busy world is hushed and the fever of life is done'—yes, go ahead, Dennis." Paul finished the prayer at a fast clip. Dennis was already halfway down the aisle.

Paul had made friends with Dennis and his cousin Horatio on a street near by, and they had come back to the yard to play ball. From then on they came daily, usually winding up in church at the regular service. Mrs. Powell made a few cracks about Canon Bryan turning over in his grave with Hottentots in the mahogany pews, but soon she took them for granted.

Honor and Pip, their blond heads barely visible above the brown wood of the pew, sat with Horatio, Dennis's spokesman in this moment of crisis. Behind them were two older Negro girls, Naomi and Louise, about thirteen. Horatio plunked himself on his knees after his request was granted, and Honor and Pip crawled in beside him. Mrs. Powell and I sat directly behind them; she could contain herself no longer. "I declare, young man," she said, tapping Horatio on the shoulder with her cane, "there's places for everything, and the church ain't a place for scootin' around the floor or excusing yourself for the toilet."

Horatio's skinny body had turned with the rap of the cane, his eyes widened, and he scampered wordless down the aisle after Dennis, followed by Louise. "Thoth boyth," she lisped to Naomi as she left, "they don't know they'th in church." The remaining heads were bowed again, and Paul said the final prayer. The evening service was over and we filed out—the little children, Naomi, composed and quiet in her dark dress and straightened hair, Mrs. Powell, and I.

The yard was full of early-evening shadows, long and angular, stalking the tenement wall and the grass, already patchy from summer use. Dennis and Horatio—inseparable, it seemed—were playing ball while a lecture on church manners from Louise rained down on their heads. We all stood around on the sidewalk for a while, and Mrs. Powell sat on the lych-gate bench with Lucille, the three little boys digging in the dirt at her feet. A bunch of teen-age Negro boys whom Paul knew slightly came close to the fence and stood talking and laughing. When we went over to greet them, Lucille gathered her children and toys and moved quickly into her house. She was able to sit out a sidewalk game of Dennis and Horatio, but adolescent Negro boys frightened her, and she invariably left.

Negro children had begun to hang around more and more, looking for someone to talk to or play with. Many households had no man at home, and those that did consisted of two working parents. Unemployment was very apparent among those in their late teens. Streets were filled with young people with nothing to do. Our block became their gathering place, especially in the early evening. We had spent a month in Jersey City, and all our new Negro acquaintances were under eighteen. In these early days Paul, Kim, and Bob met Negro adults only through the children. "You gonna love my aunt" (pronounced "ont"), Louise would say, tugging Paul's hand to walk three more blocks. "Pleath, Father," she would lisp, "the house be right around the next two cornerth."

At first, no parent came on his own to the rectory, and any introduction was a random one made on the street by one of the children. An encounter in front of Howdy's candy store, brought Bob in contact with a Negro minister, a young Baptist named Lewis. A new religious census in his possession confirmed what was becoming clearer and clearer, and what we had already read in another report when we were still in New York: the so-called unchurched (those without any formal religious connections) in lower Jersey City were an almost entirely Negro group, with a Puerto Rican section just emerging. Lewis urged Paul, Kim, and Bob to make use of the census information, and Grace Church became more involved in what was not yet called the ghetto.

The poorer the street, the more apt it was to be Negro. There were vast all-Negro areas in lower Jersey City, and a few of the white streets within a small radius of us contained two or three Negro tenements on the block.

Dennis and Naomi lived across the hall from one another in one such building two blocks down Second Street. Crumbling walls and halls, landlords who have no interest in the tenant except financial, garbage that stays around longer than in other neighborhoods, the ever-present reality of eviction for nonpayment of rent, the scarred walls from a stove fire of long ago, the frozen toilet, the odor of cheap wine—these made up Dennis's and Naomi's world. From my upstairs window I could see a vegetable garden, covered garbage cans, a plastic swimming pool or two. Dennis and Naomi had no such treasures in their backyards.

None of us knew very much about the lives of the children, who treated us alternately as adored Santa Clauses or as fearsome figures whose glance they could not meet. We knew of typical urban housing from our experiences in New

York, but we were ignorant of all the constant fears, harassments, and discomforts the day can hold for someone who is very poor—eviction, fire, insults, unemployment, rejection, hunger, cold—the list is long. Books of the period did not talk of smelly hallways, nor did newspapers report marches on City Hall to complain of improper garbage collection. In the late forties and early fifties, "antipoverty" was not a term. Poverty itself had little news value.

Negro children, when they first came around to see where those "new white ministers" lived, were very elusive. They played in our yard but refused for weeks to come in the house, instead pressing noses against our kitchen windows as we ate, giggling when we spoke, or scooting back to the sidewalk when we went to the door to ask them in. We reacted to this first experience of race in our midst with varying degrees of overcompensation. We forgave Dennis his games with the lids of garbage cans. We overlooked Louise's grabbing the cupcake from the kitchen table after she had finally screwed up enough courage to cross the threshold. Once the barrier of our front door was braved though, they quickly came to feel at ease in our kitchen. Each day when they all left, Dennis would say, "When you gonna bring Honor and Pip over to my house?"

I was a little nervous when I left the security of our block, but I had promised Dennis we'd come, and my children were dying to visit him. We moved at an uneven pace down the hot street, Honor and Pip jogging along on their tricycles. Two doors down from us was a Polish sea captain, acorn-brown and wrinkled, almost always at his first-floor window or on his stoop, with a visored cap on his head and a pipe in his mouth, looking off into the distance. One foot was deformed, and he wore a huge boot on it that looked as though it could be used for all manner of brutality. My children remember it with terror. He had never learned English, and his silence was interrupted only by sporadic and incomprehensible bursts of rage about the activities at Grace Church that disturbed his haven. But this day he must have been dozing, and we walked by unseen. The first intersection we had to cross was in front of the bleak yellow brick of St. Mary's Church, its huge, concrete flight of steps rising from the sidewalk. On the opposite corner, our undertaker friend of the heavy Italian accent shrugged recognition as we passed. A neat row of two-story houses ran for a block or so, then ended abruptly. Between them and the tall tenement where Naomi and Dennis lived was a vacant lot, covered with bits of glass, newspapers, and rusting tin cans. Our tricycle pattern became less random, and we picked our way through the glass that was scattered here and there on the sidewalk. Two skinny girls were skipping rope. They were not children I knew, and they bleated a slow "ma'am" when I spoke to them. I pulled the tricycles over near the steps and told the girls we were going to visit Dennis Smith upstairs. They dropped their rope and stood and gaped at us in disbelief. Honor and Pip were too little to be concerned about anything except the prospect of seeing Dennis. For the first time, I began wondering why I had imagined Dennis Smith's mother wanted this family onslaught from me. But all the doubts vanished when Dennis screamed delightedly from an upstairs window, "Here comes Miz Moore! Come on up! Hi, Pip! Hi, Honor!" Moments later, Naomi was at an adjacent window, waving. They both came to the doorway to escort us up. There was no door, and the hallway was dark except for a twenty-five-watt bulb hanging toward the rear near the stairwell. My children held my hands. I grew accustomed to the lack of light and made out the row of mailboxes shoulder-high. One was broken and the metal case hung open like the jaw of some deformed fish.

The children adored Dennis and clattered eagerly up the dark stairway after him. Naomi climbed with me. She said nothing. I wondered if her silence were not a questioning of my reaction to the airless hallways, the blaring radios and voices behind the closed doors. A cat slid by our legs and we laughed. "Get out, cat," Naomi said. I followed Dennis and my children, already at the Smiths' door.

It opened into the kitchen, a small square room with an electric stove and a refrigerator. A bulb on a cord in the center of the ceiling had a long brown spiral of flypaper attached to it, where flies, in various stages of death agony, kept up a ceaseless buzz that made my flesh tickle. I turned away to look in the room beyond that overlooked the street. Between the two windows were a brown, metal oil stove and a couple of large upholstered chairs, one of them covered with a brown Army blanket.

Dennis ran ahead. "Mamma, this is the Moores." I shook hands and Mrs. Smith welcomed me. She bent over to tell the children how cute they were, and with sudden shyness Honor and Pip moved closer to me as I sat in the armchair. Each of them touched my leg with one outstretched hand in that grave way small children have. They waited and looked around.

Mrs. Smith was of medium height, heavy and cheerful. She told me she had been born in the South, had come years ago to Jersey with her grandmother to visit with cousins, and had never left. "It was hard," she said, "to get a job." She worked in a commercial laundry, but this was her day off. She left for work at five in the morning, when the children were still sleeping, and earned the regular laundry wage of sixty-five cents an hour. Mr. Smith worked nights and was in bed now. The other children—there were eight of them in all—were out playing—maybe I'd met her girls skipping rope?

Naomi came in from across the hall with her mother, who was carrying a child. Mrs. Smith introduced us. "Mrs. Moore from the church—Alma Trotter, my neighbor." Naomi stood at the window, and her mother sat in the other armchair, still holding the little boy. He appeared to be about four.

The drooling mouth, the vacant gaze, the brief convulsive movements of his body showed that something was very wrong. It was not explained. Mrs. Trotter was quiet like Naomi but less self-conscious. She mentioned the hot weather we'd been having and then spoke softly to the little boy. He smiled delightedly, and his body moved in slight jerks in response to his mother's words. Sometimes his too-stiff fingers, usually arched idly over his thin chest, would reach up toward his mother's blue beads. I asked the women more about their families, and they told me how grateful they were for the church. It was a place for their children to keep out of trouble, they said.

Would we ever break through, I wondered, to any real communication? It was like a movie: I was the white woman talking, asking polite questions; Mrs. Smith and Mrs. Trotter were the Negroes nodding in agreement and pronouncing nice phrases. Everything seemed intensified; it was as if the void between white and black America had a physical presence in that room at that moment. I began to feel hot inside. Thoughts tumbled: guilt that we were free to leave Jersey City as we had been free to come; needless guilt, another part of me said. I remembered a saint's words, "Forgive us our charity. . . ." There was that phoniness again.

I asked the two mothers to visit our church, and, of course, they said yes. I didn't know yet that "yes" was always the answer. I marveled at Mrs. Trotter's acceptance of the pitiful little boy, at the hopes she held for her children though aware that for her not much was going to change. "It's just the way it is," she said over and over. "God doesn't give you more than you can bear."

I glanced at Naomi during the conversation. She was polishing her nails with the belt of her cotton dress. It was hard to figure out what she was thinking. Dennis clattered down the stairs with us when we left, and Naomi waved from an upstairs window.

Gradually, Dennis and Naomi became my main sources of information. What they didn't tell me, Louise, usually giggling and with less accuracy, filled in.

It took more than the first summer, and more than a few confidences from the children, for me to realize that, despite occasional integregation, "white" meant "authority" to the Negroes we knew. In 1951 the first Negro was made a sergeant in the Jersey City police force, but a white cop would, as a rule, be the one to catch Dennis loitering on a corner, playing ball or sidewalk games. "Move along, nigger boy," he'd say, and Dennis learned to dart quickly behind a truck or down an alley, calling the cop under his breath all the words he had learned on the street.

In the fall, I found out that Dennis and Horatio's third-grade teacher was white, although almost the whole class was Negro. (Most of the white children in the school district went to parochial school.) She and her fellow teachers were old-fashioned and hardworking; the equipment was sturdy and unimaginative, but there was enough of it; the halls and classrooms were well lit and clean; report cards, devoid of psychological evaluations, graded with finality a child's work all the way from excellent to failing. The school administration was confident of its ability and proud of the education it had been delivering unchanged for many years. No one in authority had yet realized that the textbooks were in no way expressive of the background of the deprived Negroes or Puerto Ricans who were enrolling in the school in increasing numbers.

The teacher tried hard in her own way, but she had no notion why Horatio and Dennis were often listless and sleepy. She didn't know that they rarely had a real breakfast, that Dennis's father worked nights and was asleep when Dennis left, that his mother worked days and was gone when he was still in bed, that sometimes in Horatio's house there were no jobs and no money. She had assumed, I'm sure, as normal school had expressed it to her when she worked for her teaching degree in 1928, that reading skills could be related to the home background. But the wonderful, half scary stories that Dennis's mother told him about snakes and swamps and memories of corn roasts were nothing like the stories Dennis was expected to learn and relate to at school. Dick and Jane, in the school reader, had white faces; their father went to work in what looked to Dennis like a Sunday suit, drove home in a car, and parked it near green grass. Opposite that page was a picture of him calling up the stairs, "Dick and Jane, I'm home. How is the new puppy?" That hat in his hand was what people wore in the movies. He was calling Dick and Jane from a bright doorway. In Dennis's doorway you barely recognized people, it was that dark. And Dennis's father never wore a hat or a Sunday suit, except to church, and Dennis could remember that only twice. Dick and Jane's puppy was about the size of the cats that stalked up the stairway so quiet you didn't even know they were there. It was brown like the rat his father killed with his bare hands when it jumped into the baby's crib.

Dennis's teacher, Miss Murray, knew her pupils' homes weren't the same as the home she had grown up in, but she didn't know quite what to do about it. She said as much to the children. "When Daddy comes home from work, ask him to help you with your lessons—that is, if he has time," she told Dennis over and over. Dennis never remembered his coming home from work, it was so early in the morning. Mostly he saw his father in bed, or listening to the radio. He asked him once for money for the movies, he told me, and his father threw a quarter to him and said, "Git, boy, I'm tired." So after that Dennis asked his mother. Sometimes she would find money for the movies, but she didn't have enough schooling to be able to help him with his homework.

Miss Murray worried about her class. "The Southern background is a real drawback," she told me when I met her, "and I'm not a bit prejudiced."

Naomi, Dennis, Louise, and Horatio all lived in four-story tenements with seven or so other families in their buildings. They rented the narrow railroad flats from landlords who bought up two or three buildings at a time, lived in other parts of the city, or the suburbs, and only came around to collect the rent. Most of them were white, and all the mothers Dennis knew were afraid of them.

He used to mimic his mother when their landlord was at her door: "Yessir, yessir, I have the money ready. Fetch it boy, from on the dresser. Move sharp. The landlord ain't got all day," and Dennis did an exaggerated curtsy. His mother always talked bold, except to white men, so Dennis couldn't understand why she acted funny with this landlord man, since he was light brown. Never anything but "Yes, sir," "No, sir," "Please, sir," like she acted with the white school principal. Mr. Felipe, the landlord man, had a funny accent; West Indian, Mamma said, and he had a wooden leg. Maybe that's what made everyone act different with him, Dennis decided. It stuck out of his pant leg, bulged out round and shiny like the rat's eyes after his father choked it. The leg rapped on the stairs when Mr. Felipe came up for the rent money. He always called Dennis's little brother "nigger baby" and threw pennies at him on the floor while his mother counted out the rent.

All the children in the house were a little afraid of him, but instead of saying they were frightened they imitated the way he walked, especially the awkward way he had of helping his leg up each step with his hand. Sometimes they would hide behind the first floor stairwell to watch him limping down. One time Dennis told me about hiding there alone. Naomi was following Mr. Felipe on the stairs with a big pail of trash to put out for her mother.

"Set down that big bundle, pretty little lady," Mr. Felipe said, catching Naomi's arm at the bottom landing. Dennis's body was behind the stairs, but he told me he leaned out and watched the two figures outlined in the dim hallway. The landlord held Naomi tight by her hands. That was when Dennis heard her cry. He watched Mr. Felipe, his wooden leg way out to the side, push her against the wall, but he let her go when she screamed. Dennis kept his eye on him after she ran upstairs. It looked as if Mr. Felipe's leg was stuck to the wall. He had to steer it with his hand. Then after he got it turned around straight, he pushed at the door with his hand, and it swung shut behind him.

I asked Dennis if he had told his mother about the incident. "She'd holler that I was peekin'," he answered. Instead, he said, he went to his mother's kitchen—flies were buzzing around a pot on the stove—and turned on the radio real loud. His father came to the door in an undershirt.

"Turn off that noise. I'm sleepin'," he yelled. Dennis snapped off the radio. Everything was quiet except for the buzzing of the flies. Then Dennis said he just forgot about it.

Paul told me later of meeting Mr. Felipe on rent collection day at the same address. Mrs. Trotter introduced them in the upstairs hall. Mr. Felipe was a *Porgy and Bess* character, with his light brown skin, his black shirt and pants, his primitive wooden leg. Paul said he couldn't help feeling that his pant leg was cut extravagantly wide and even a little short to show off the false limb in all its homemade horror. The two men left together. Mr. Felipe seemed to enjoy the length of time it took him to thump the three flights to the street ahead of Paul. "You new in the neighborhood, Father?" he questioned between the sharp raps of his leg on the wooden stairs. Before Paul could answer, the landlord's voice came up the stairwell again, suddenly hoarse and twangy. "There's only one reason white men be in a house like this, and that's looking for black meat," and he laughed loudly. Paul reminded him about the broken stairs, said good-bye, and they parted.

Twice a year a white Democratic political worker called on everyone in that block. Naomi told me about the time he came to persuade her mother to move into the new project where he said the rent would stay the same. Naomi had never heard any white person talk so nice, and Louise, with her usual gift of gab, said as far as *she* was concerned he sounded like what some folks told her about President Roosevelt. Naomi described how he took off his hat when he came in and put it real gentle on the arm of the chair, how he shook Mrs. Trotter's hand, introduced himself—"Mr. Norman's the name"—and pulled candies out of his pocket. "I bet you're not too big for candy, are you?" He laughed and gave her some chocolate.

But he had made Naomi nervous. "Reminded me of that landlord man rubbin' up my legs," she said.

Louise shrieked with laughter, then words came pouring out. She was as intent on my getting her story as she was in registering strong dissent with Naomi. They were both in my kitchen, and Louise leaned back against the refrigerator. "So what's so wrong with that, girl?" *She* did things like that with boys, sometimes in the alley at night, and *she* liked it. Once even, she did it with a little boy about ten years old, no bigger than Dennis. He got it real stiff and stuck it in her. That's when her father caught her and beat her with a whip. And as if that wasn't enough, he washed her mouth out with brown soap and told her she'd grow up crazy like Naomi's brother. And all because she'd done it with that little kid.

Naomi grew exasperated. "You might like it, girl, but I still be scared when I think of Mr. Felipe holding on to me." Louise snickered, her hand over her mouth, but Naomi wasn't through. All she'd had to do as she held the candy in her hand was close her eyes and she could remember Mr. Felipe's body pressed hard against her and his breath so close to her, like it was part of his mouth and her mouth, sweet-smelling and sour-smelling—taste and smell all mixed up together. And then suddenly Naomi was quiet.

"What wrong with you, girl?" questioned Louise. "You just bashful?"

Naomi smiled briefly, a little patronizingly, and went on with her account. Mr. Norman had sat talking to her mother as nice as can be about the project. It was brand new, built with Federal funds, he said, and if she could wait till after the election in November, he knew he could get her three nice rooms by Christmas. Naomi could have a bed of her own; she wouldn't have to sleep with her mother and little brother. "Remember, Mrs. Trotter, November third I'll send one of my workers round or I'll come myself and take you to the polls. We'll even tell you how to vote." He laughed and then grew suddenly very serious. Naomi described his leaning forward, pulling his pants up a little from his ankles. "I'll let you in on a big secret, Mrs. Trotter, you and this nice girl of yours. You won't have a chance at rooms in the project if you don't vote for my candidate." He stood up. "And my candidate has your interest at heart." He shook hands with Naomi. "Don't wait till that candy melts all over that pretty dress of yours," he said.

By Christmas they had three rooms in the housing project. The rough plaster walls were painted light brown, and the floors were concrete. In the beginning, some of their neighbors were white, but within a few years it was all Negro, and another project was all white.

Whites ran the movie theaters, too. On Saturday nights, if they couldn't get fifteen cents at home, Dennis and Horatio would sneak into the theater known as "The Itch." The white girl who ushered always caught them and dragged them out. "If you weren't so damn little, I'd turn you over to the cops," she said at first. But they kept doing it, so she did. The cops said they wanted to scare them some, and they slapped them around, called them "jigaboos" and used a lot of dirty words before they let them go.

For the teacher, the policeman, the landlord, the ward heeler, the lady at the movie theater, the Negro child was "a colored kid." That was always the phrase. I had seen parents in my childhood world too busy for their children or their children's friends, careless of the hurts that fester behind wide eyes. I thought I knew of prejudice; after all, I'd read Richard Wright–*Black Boy, Native Son,* and the rest. But I had not realized that brown skin could cancel all the other qualities–the Naomi-ness–of the straight-bodied girl who sat in my kitchen, or the enthusiasm of Dennis, who played with my children.

Months later, when Dennis was baptized, he came into the house afterwards. There were beads of sweat on his upper lip, although the weather was cool. I was touched by the way he looked, so anxious and excited. "Do I really belong now?" he asked.

"Yes," I answered. The moment was brief–his concern was racial rather than religious–and the profoundness of it lasted longer for me than for him. He dashed off, slamming the front door, and played a wild game of tag behind the garbage cans.

VII *"It Used To Be So Quiet Here"*

The first time they appeared, the three white boys stood in the back of the parish hall, looking around. It was immediately obvious, from their sixteen-year-olds' disdain for the television audience, mostly women and children, that they were not going to stay.

"They're bad," Howdy said to Paul when he spotted them "—in trouble with the cops, truants, screwing girls at the movies. Eddie's folks have been here forever, but Nathan and Billy are new since the war, come from somewhere else in Jersey after the factories closed down."

The boys' heavy shoes had sounded in unison as they walked in. Now they stood tugging at the bottoms of their shiny jackets, or with thumbs hooked into their belts. Paul walked back to greet them. They shook hands awkwardly, as though it were a tribal custom of a far-off generation from which they had evolved.

We had known others like them in the Chelsea section of New York. Nurtured by the crowded city, and postwar cynicism and unemployment, they were part of the mobs of rebellious boys who roamed the streets in angry confusion, suspicions of and suspected by a world whose rewards lay beyond their grasp.

Later in the week, the three boys showed up again in their

duck-tail haircuts, sateen jackets, and skintight pants—symbols of defiance. I watched them lean their restless bodies against the back wall of the parish house. Within seconds Mrs. Powell was on her feet in the darkened hall, the television program still rattling on. She gave the group of boys a wide berth, beckoned Paul with cane aloft and, lowering her voice, said to him, "It's one thing for Father Flanagan to build a Boys Town, but the likes of you better stick to praying—them boys got police records."

Paul laughed and answered her the way he had responded in so many other similar situations: "The boys are part of the same neighborhood as you are. They came here of their own will. We'll try to get to know them—maybe there'll be something for them around here."

"Like the church safe, mebbe?" Mrs. Powell questioned wryly.

With Paul close behind, she swept over close to the boys and gave them the full benefit of a Powell confrontation—legs slightly apart, left hand jabbing at the lavender straw hat, right hand on the cane. The words came like buckshot. "See you mind your knitting, young men."

The boys looked startled, then embarrassed. "Yes, ma'am." Nathan spoke for the trio, and Mrs. Powell drew a deep, prideful breath and returned to her seat.

Paul stood against the concrete wall near Nathan. The boys had apparently expected to be kicked out, and I could see they were glad enough to carry on a conversation with Paul while keeping an eye on the Western movie on the small screen. Nathan was heavyset, dark haired, with a general air of naughty bravado, as though he were trying to look like one of those photographs in post offices of men whose capture means a huge reward. He told Paul his father worked from time to time in a radio repair shop, always yelled at him, and had slugged him ever since he could remember. He had a mother who doted and worried. "The old lady works at the can company. Pushes a piece of solder all day." To illustrate, he bent and unbent his index finger with deliberate timing on the wall. "She's done it for years, but she's too softhearted to quit and get the old man off his ass."

Billy and Eddie said little, but agreed with Nathan and his bits of philosophy: "Church is for women, school is for quittin', the city is for nothin'." They stayed until long after the rest of the audience had left and a tiny pinpoint of light whizzed into nothingness on the television screen. "Looks like a goddam cat's eye," mumbled Eddie.

When Paul came to bed he described their conversation in detail, and told me the boys had promised to return. Back they came on successive nights, their talk shifting from stormy, passionate denunciations of what they would have called, had they known the term, the inner city, to boyish stories of baseball prowess. Eddie, blue-eyed and pink-cheeked, was a clown and con man, and still served daily Mass at St. Aloysius' Church a few blocks away. "I steal pennies from the plate right under the Father's nose," he said with his one-sided smile. In every job the three of them did together, and their operations were still relatively innocent, Eddie was left behind to con the victim. "Nathan and Billy played hide-and-seek up the aisles of the A & P with the stuff we lifted, while I was left talking to a lady customer who seen us do it. I gave her the thank-you treatment about some booties she knit for the old lady when she dropped my new kid brother at Margaret Hague Hospital. When we was all three a block away, she was still there smiling her fool face off."

Billy, the last member of the trio, exceptionally even-featured and handsome, held his cards close. What we knew about him we learned from the others. He was the only one who was fatherless. He had already been to court endless times for truancy and stealing, while the others were, despite Howdy's remarks, relative novices. Billy was always after them to get started on a big job—like breaking into a store on the Avenue—but they dragged their feet.

"The old lady'd drop dead," said Eddie.

Within days, Paul's relationship with the boys had developed to the point where they spent less time boasting of their exploits and began to press him to help them start a baseball team. It was Nathan who insisted on it, assuring Paul he could find players and opponents. He came early in the morning and late in the evening to report his progress and often arrived halfway through one of the daily services, dropping on his knees next to Paul with a great thump, announcing developments in a dramatic whisper—"Grabowski says he'll pitch."

Kim, Paul, and Bob were already spending part of each day in the parish hall supervising an informal recreational program. They had put up a basketball hoop, discouraged tag, and hoped the children, who they knew would stay, would also remain entertained. But Paul's new project was a more ambitious one, mainly because there were no baseball diamonds in the area and the players always needed transportation.

Bob and Kim bought a thin red volume, *Baseball for Everyone,* by Joe DiMaggio, and donated it to Paul, who was rather sensitive as the newly crowned manager. He hotly denied that his team was anything but a howling success. He did have problems, however, besides transportation. Grabowski, it turned out, was a red-hot pitcher but had to be dragged from his bed in a fourth-floor walk-up apartment each morning when Paul and Nathan made their sortie in the station wagon to pick up stragglers for daily practice. After a couple of weeks, Eddie got a job in a grocery store and dropped out, and Billy was sent to the county juvenile center for a week because he had stolen his mother's radio and pawned it. (When Billy appeared in court, we had our introduction to the *Going My Way* approach of the well-intentioned Juvenile Court judge: "Go to church and talk to Father Moore, and everything will be fine.") Others came and went, and the team limped along through the summer. Whatever it may have done for the boys, baseball made us aware of the absence of downtown playground space, the lack of organized recreation for teen-agers, and the interminable length of city summers. And, through Billy, it put us in touch with the law.

Dennis and Horatio were often on the stoop when I came down to fix breakfast. By noon, Naomi had finished chores for her mother and would come to sit at the lych-gate with her scatterbrained girl friend, Louise. Louise chattered constantly in a decided lisp, played ball with the boys, and threw pebbles at the telephone poles, while Naomi, beautiful and brooding, sat and watched. Naomi, barely into her teens, fussed with her nails, straightened her hair, and thought before she spoke; Louise, at the same age, was a nature girl, clean if the spirit or her big sister moved her, covered with dirt if they didn't. Louise told me that her sister took care of her because she had no mother, that her father only came home now and then, and that she had six younger brothers. She took to the trappings of religion as if it were a new sidewalk game, parading down Second Street with some local five-year-olds in tow, singing hyms at the top of her lungs. Her high point was an intricate game of skip rope, in which she chanted,

> "O Thacred Victim opening wide
> The gate of heaven to man below"

in what she called her prayer voice, twirling the rope in triple time. Naomi managed the other end, and a third girl jumped in and out. The girls wanted as much attention as the boys at Grace Church, but for the moment their program was limited to a humdrum club of fifteen girls, with

Louise and Naomi as president and secretary; I was adviser or, as Louise described it, "thponthor." We planned outings, had short-lived cooking and sewing projects. Our weekly meetings in the rectory kitchen were dominated by Louise's constant double refrain: "Will the meeting pleath come to order?" "Will you pleath thut up?"

Occasionally Paul and I indulged in feelings of self-satisfaction about the unprejudiced attitudes and the atmosphere of democracy which our small children were absorbing, it seemed to us, by osmosis. The naturalness of their friendships was, we felt, the key factor. But there were other moments that brought us up short. One occurred on an evening in midsummer. We all heard it. An unmistakable small Moore voice came from the front yard. "Some goddam nigger stole my shubbel!" Paul and I were eating supper with Kim and Bob, and the kitchen window was open to catch the first evening breeze. Mrs. Powell, her lavender hat reposing on our refrigerator, sat on a stool drinking sherry while we ate.

She downed the wine in one gulp and walked to the window. "I told you folks you shouldn't open up your yard to every Tom, Dick, and Harry. Now you've got yourselves a couple of foulmouthed kids." We all laughed, Paul and I somewhat hollowly, as we left the table to see what was the matter.

We found Pip kicking angrily at a tuft of what was left of the grass. "Some goddam nigger stole my shubbel!" He was repeating the phrase with the persistence of the very young. Oblivious to his wailing, his sister was plunging a spoon delightedly into the dry dirt. Whoever had been the culprit had fled, and Pip and Honor were alone except for Lucille. She was leaning, back to us, on the iron fence that separated our yard from the sidewalk, and she turned her head to look as we approached the children. Through the blond hair hanging forward and close to her cheek, we heard her voice, brimming with disdain and triumph.

"Can't trust those colored kids," she said.

Paul hoisted Pip to his shoulder, his grief now only a gulp, and they went up the steps to the rectory.

"What happened?" I asked Honor.

"One of those kids took the shovel and ran with it, but Pip threw it at him first." I decided to leave well enough alone, and we dropped the subject. Later we laughed about the magnificent training we were giving our children for life in the wide, wide world.

At that time, some of the regular television crowd often would come around to talk while we were eating supper, or new people like the Coreys would arrive early, anxious to be the ones to get the keys and open up the parish hall. We could always hear the Coreys coming. "Frank," Mae would call, "don't forget to ring the bell—it's not Grand Central Station. Children, keep quiet."

"What makes you think I don't have no manners?" Or, "Don't you think my mother brought me up right?" Frank would challenge.

The bell would ring and we would call "Come in" from the kitchen table. "Surprise!" said Frank invariably, his family crowding around him in the tiny hallway. Frank had the florid young-old face one associates with jockeys, and his pants were bunched over his hips and around his waist as though they had been tied with a string or he had suddenly lost weight. Mae was Hawaiian. "Part of me is on the Islands—that's what I tell the children," she often said. She had a faintly exotic look, long since rouged over, and her black little-girl bob hung lifeless. The four children were pale and tugged at each other irritably.

One night the Coreys arrived earlier than usual. The children stood self-consciously around the door to the kitchen, their brown eyes darting from mother to father to the floor. Frank and Mae pulled two chairs up to the table to join us.

"Just thought we'd drop by," explained Frank, "and give you a hand opening up the hall. The kids were driving the wife crazy—'What time can we go over to church?' all day long—too hot to stay in two rooms, and the wife has no patience since Davie died."

"Davie, our oldest, passed away last Christmas, just turned fourteen," Mae explained as though she had never told us before. "A brain tumor. He kept having these headaches, and then he was unconscious. We didn't have a church then, so he was laid out in the parlor on the Avenue."

Every time they came, she talked of Davie. Frank added details and sometimes disputed her version, but Mae was the chief spokesman. She told of his first tooth, his first day of school, the day "he stole a kiss from a little colored kid with pigtails—he didn't know any better, but the teacher hollered at him."

"It was a Tuesday night he took sick, remember? Have you got a match, Frank? My God, you oughta carry them with you—see, he was hiding them in his hip pocket all the time. Scratch the match—hurry, will you?" Mae chided.

Each time she spoke of him, she cried and asked Frank to light her a cigarette. It was oddly tender the way he did it, cupping her chin in his red, trembling hand and helping her firm the cigarette between her lips.

"No, Mae, it was a Wednesday—you think I'd ever forget a day like that?" Frank corrected her with dogged patience. "I was reading the paper. Davie came into the kitchen and said, 'Dad, I can't go to school with the kind of headache I got,' and I looked up—it was Wednesday's paper, I know that for sure. It's funny the things you remember—'Wednesday,' it said there on the front page. 'March 4, snow flurries likely,' and how it snowed! When the ambulance came, even the driver was talking about it—and he was an experienced ambulance driver. 'Can you imagine,' he said when he come up the stairs, 'snow in March, and spring only weeks off.' He wouldn't have talked so light if he'd known how bad off Davie was. He was an experienced man, and when he come in the room, he took one look at Davie and said to us real nice, 'You do have a sick boy on your hands.' "

"He wasn't so experienced like you say, Frank," Mae broke in, "and a mother always knows. When he carried Davie down those stairs, it was bump, bump, bump, and him with that headache. It done a lot of damage, if you ask me."

"Mae, you got it all wrong. He knew it was a coma. He told me, 'You gotta rush these coma cases—operating's the only hope.' When Davie fainted there, he never was right again—that was the start of the coma, Mae," Frank reminded her.

Mae, tearful, lit another cigarette from the stub she held in her hand. "He never spoke again, and before we knew it—it *was* before we knew it, that quick, wasn't it, Frank?—he'd passed on and was buried. And they wouldn't even let me dress him. Just a chance he had meningitis as well as the brain tumor—contagious, they said. They wouldn't let his own mother touch him, but they put the blue suit on when I asked them. He was growing so fast, wasn't he, Frank? Another month and he'd have needed a new blue suit." The tears were on her cheeks now.

"Honey, you exaggerate. That suit fitted him fine. He'd have used it for a long time. You don't think right about that day." Frank handed her a handkerchief, but she shook her head.

"Frank, when he was laid out in the funeral parlor I can remember saying to the other children, 'How would Davie feel with his ankles showing under those fancy pants?' And Dolores said, 'Mamma, I can't look, I'm scared.' "

I had been brought up in a world where the physical aspects of dying were not mentioned, let alone the minute descriptions of suffering that Mae was driven to share. Her constant confidences revealing the most private face of grief alternately touched and repelled me. I didn't know then that they were what kept her going. Each night there was talk about *the* job or *no* job, Mae puffing on her cigarette as she spoke. "Frank got work today—he'll get paid every other week." But his jobs never seemed to last that long. There was always a day or two with no work, then a new job.

Once he hauled in a huge sack of Ajax cleanser and presented it to me after a day of work in a Hoboken factory. "They give the sweepings away after they fill the cans. The powder in the sweepings is just as good as the can that costs thirty-nine cents." He heaved the sack into the kitchen. A corner of it split, and a puff of gritty powder settled on the floor.

Limpetlike, the Coreys attached themselves to our household, sucking strength, it seemed, from this very kitchen where they sat so interminably. The children would drink lemonade and Frank and Mae coffee before they all went over for television. Afterwards, they stood on the street till everyone had gone. "We'd better get the children to bed," Frank would say finally, and Mae would add, "Come on, you kids, don't we have anything better to do than hang around here?"

Horace and Mary, brother and sister, were other suppertime callers. They were both retarded. With the terrible diamond-bright innocence of the feebleminded, they told anyone who would listen each and every problem. Horace was clever with his hands and could fix anything. Time and time again we found him a job, but he would run aimless fingers through his red, tousled hair and ruin his chances by telling his employer he couldn't sign his name; or, if he was able to stick at the job, there would sooner or later be a task that was too much for him, and he would be back at the rectory, grinning and unemployed. He called me "Sister." "Sister Moore," he would say after a job ended, "could Father call the employment for me again?"

Listening to his sister, Mary, was like hearing a ghastly joke and being ashamed afterwards that you had laughed. "The hardest thing," she told us, "is to give it up. Horace says I'll get in trouble. He says I'll have a baby if I keep on doing it. Horace says it's worse since the sailor I'm doing it with isn't my real boy friend. Don't you think it's right, Father, that I'm giving it up?"

Every evening that first summer they came over early to sweep the parish hall before television. Then Mary would chat with us or with the Coreys, and Horace, with his usual pocketful of tools, would use the time to patch a rectory window, tighten the oven door, or fix anything else that was in need of repair. If Mrs. Powell was there, she gave him directions. At the end of the evening they would straighten the rows of chairs, sweep up again, and come to say good night. "I'll iron his shirt real good when he goes to the employment office in the morning," Mary would say, leaning back heavily on her heel to catch her reflection in the wide strip of chrome on the refrigerator door. Then she would comb her red hair and puff it with her long fingernails, and they would leave, hand in hand, for the boardinghouse in Hoboken.

The problem, in July, of not enough people coming by, had been supplanted, in August, by the problem of what to do with so many of them. With the influx, a few inhabitants of our block reverted to their original hostile mood and petitioned Bishop Washburn that we be removed. The message, written in green ball-point pen, read that the ministers had stirred up the lovely, peaceful church so that it was noisy on Second Street all week long. The married minister, it continued, allowed his children and others to play on the once cared for grass, so that there were large bare spots. The only flaw in the petition was that the fifty signatures were written in blocks of only three different handwritings. The Bishop advised that we disregard it as he had.

Nevertheless, Howdy kept passing along complaints when we stopped at the candy store for the *Jersey Journal.*

"Some people's calling it a nigger church," he reported, wrapping up his words as expressionlessly as he did the evening paper. Neighbors with whom we had had reasonably affable truces began to turn away when we passed. In one of the few times Lucille spoke to me during this period, she said the gossip was that the Bishop was going to buy up all the houses on the block and rent them to Negroes. I assured her that the Bishop had no interest in speculating in real estate, but church activities did need more space and I was sure that would be the motive of any purchase. She nodded, unconvinced, and looked at her fingernails. "It used to be so quiet here," she said, "only a month ago." And then she avoided more conversation.

The old guard questioned us, too. Mrs. Hogan looked down her nose at Naomi and Dennis in the pews. But it was not only race. She barely nodded at some of the church's new white members like Mae and Frank Corey, who found their way with obvious difficulty through the sonorous hymns and the Elizabethan English of the prayers. It was hard for her to accept these changes on Sundays; it was just as hard for her to understand why the stone tower she had known for years should cast its shadow all week long on Dennis's ball playing and Frank and Mae's comings and goings.

Late at night when the last caller had gone, when the stoops were empty of Lucille and the tricycles, the Polish sea captain shrieking vengeance on the interlopers, and Mr. D'Agostino objecting to our theology, we four would talk around the kitchen table. We laughed over the too-easy philosophizing about a city parish we had done the year before, and talked about the people on Second Street who had come into our lives in such a flood. Perhaps we were callous about our property-wary neighbors and their fears, but the open sores in the lives of all those who had come for help were so real that they could not be ignored. And so we went on, opening the parish hall every night, binding as best we could the wounds of city living, and growing more involved.

At this point, with more and more people coming to Second Street each day and with very little to occupy them, Louise introduced Paul to Mrs. Hyde. Louise was anxious for us to know not only her family and friends but also her fleeting acquaintances—a group which sometimes seemed to include about a quarter of the city—so it didn't take her long to engineer Paul's meeting with her downstairs neighbor. "Mrs. Hyde be really thmart," she said. "Her kidth be thmart-aleck, but anywayth I keep telling about Grathe Church and Father Moore."

Mrs. Hyde was tall, angular, attractive, and astringent but friendly. She had a well-paying job as a secretary in New York during the day. Her Northern background and college education set her apart from her neighbors; yet because she was Negro and because any housing was scarce in the post-war period, a narrow railroad flat in a dank, depressing house on an alley was the only place she could find to live. On our still white block, with starched curtains at windows and occasional flowers at doorways, poverty appeared genteel; the building where Mrs. Hyde and Louise lived was a pocket of raw destitution with no pretense of politeness about it. The tenants on the top floor sent their garbage—coke bottles, beer cans, and all—whizzing right by Mrs. Hyde's window into the yard. There were moments when we didn't blame them —the city was so careless about garbage collection—but Mrs. Hyde believed there was no excuse and said so.

Mrs. Trotter and Mrs. Smith complained about the hallway smells, the peeling paint, the crumbling plaster, but their deepest resentments, at least in our presence, never rose to the surface. Mrs. Hyde, on the other hand, was angry. She knew why Negro slums were always the worst, the hardest to break away from, and that the larger the family, the slimmer the chance was of ever leaving. She knew that Negroes always got the poorest housing and the worst jobs, and that if they somehow escaped the ghetto, non-Negro neighbors would automatically resent them. Mrs. Hyde knew all this, and it made her angry. And she trained her two children to be angry. She taught them Negro history at home and urged her ten-year-old daughter to refuse to sing "Swing Low, Sweet Chariot" and other spirituals at school because they encouraged a stereotype of the Negro in the servitude she loathed. She taught them both that they ought to expect a lot from life, but that they would have to be tough to get it.

Right away she told Paul that she had heard of Grace Church and that she was anxious to contribute to it what abilities she had. Could she, she wondered, teach handicrafts to some of the children and adults who came around in the evenings? Paul returned overjoyed and regaled us at supper with the plans: cut down the now less-than-magic television to two nights a week, and the other weekday evenings Mrs. Hyde could run a craft program for everyone who was interested.

The next day, Dennis, Horatio, Louise, and Naomi took hastily hand-painted signs advertising the handicraft evenings to various downtown neighborhoods. The Coreys and Mary and Horace collected a vast array of odds and ends—paper bags, straws, milk-bottle tops—and begged some surplus material from local stationery and paint stores. Mae Corey, smiling in her constant and frenetic fashion, cut out letters and constructed a huge sign: "Craft Program, 7-9 P.M., Monday, Wednesday, and Friday. Come One—Come All. Everybody Welcome." Horace helped us drag out a few long trestle tables stored in the church basement and set up the chairs.

The first night was like a slightly disheveled fiesta, with feebleminded Horace as self-appointed host. When we finished supper, people were already waiting on the street for Horace to unlock the door—Dennis and his mother with all her children, Naomi, Louise, Horatio, a collection of neighbors, teen-agers from nearby blocks, even the gypsies, bedecked in bangles. After they were all seated at the long tables, Mrs. Powell made a calculated grand entrance, dropping snide remarks to no one in particular that it was all a bunch of foolishness and she had just come to watch. She sat on a folding chair on the stage at one end of the room. A few times that first evening, I came over from the rectory to look, leaving our children sleeping in the house. Mrs. Hyde was moving from table to table, and everyone—mothers, fathers, children—was folding, fitting, pasting, and pressing. She would give a word of advice here, a final pat there. Even Mrs. Powell succumbed and wrapped raffia around a cream bottle. She was thrilled with her product. "God knows, I never have any place to stick my pencil."

The program took up time, that awful burden of city summers, and that was good. Crafts and television-watching did not change anyone's life in Jersey City in 1949, but relationships had begun.

Deft as Mrs. Hyde was with pins and paper, her main interest was housing. She and Paul worked together to combat the housing crisis that resulted from the lifting of rent controls during Truman's administration. Technically this meant a twenty per cent rent increase if the landlord met certain conditions. In practice, it resulted in exploitation by the landlord, because the tenants were often ignorant of their rights. Mrs. Hyde and Paul attempted to organize Louise's aunt and the other tenants in Mrs. Hyde's building. At two different meetings, they told them that they need not pay the projected increase. Both times the tenants, all Negro, agreed to stand together, since the landlord presumably could not evict them all. When the rent fell due, everyone except Mrs. Hyde paid the illegal increase. Even with her help, we had not built enough trust. It was too soon.

VIII *"Tired, Lady?"*

Steve, our part-time sexton, had quit. His wife had been growing more and more uneasy about the changing neighborhood, and he was concerned, too. "I like you folks fine," he said over and over, "but I think you're pouring water down a rat hole—look at what they done to the lawn in the short time you been here. They don't know how to accept attention. The wife said she heard that when you give them a bathtub, they put coal in it." So Steve moved five miles away, to a town that looked, he told us proudly, like Jersey City had when he was a kid. Frank Corey, with little stamina and less in the way of standards, started cleaning the church on Saturdays.

In the house, things had not fared much better. For want of other quarters, the living room was used for meetings and Sunday School classes. We had no office space (other than our damp and leaky basement), so the living room and dining room alternated as office and counseling rooms. All visiting with old friends and people in the parish and neighborhood was done around the table in the kitchen. The constant traffic through what we grandly called "The Open Rectory" had taken its toll of the parquet floors and linoleum rugs. But the most alarming signs of the general deterioration were the pink bumps we all seemed to find in great profusion on our bodies. After conferring with the others about them, I searched the Yellow Pages of the phone book for a local exterminating firm. A voice declared that service would be immediate.

"B-bed-b-b-bugs like d-d-d-davenports," stuttered the exterminator, prodding his metal hose into the living room sofa with the vigor of a knight of old, jousting lance in hand. There was an excitement in his voice as he eagerly turned over the cushion. "They s-suck b-b-blood."

"We found them upstairs first," I told him.

Pushing high the sleeves of his shirt, tucking his weapon under his arm, he went with me up the stairs, describing during our ascent the favorite haunts of his victims: "d-davenports, s-s-sofas with s-s-soft c-corners." In New York, I had encountered "gentlemen of distinction" types in the cockroach trade, who pull up to the house in unmarked black cars, barely creasing their business suits as they discreetly aim flashlight beams into suspicious corners. My Jersey City exterminator came in a yellow truck with "Roaches-Rats-Mice-Vermin" emblazoned in huge black letters on every possible area, and he attacked his job with great relish. When we got to the third floor, his eyes were bright with anticipation.

"They l-l-like M-Murphy b-b-beds b-best of all," he said, visibly flexing his muscles and poking Bob's large pullout bed with the nozzle of his hose.

After I had said "Oh" a few times in answer to his repeated statements about the preferred lairs of bugs, I left him. Later he came down and bid me an enthusiastic farewell. "C-cash is not n-n-necessary; we send i-i-in-v-v-voices," he said as I reached for my purse. "We have a s-slogan—'Your P-p-p-problem Is Our P-pleasure.' "

Late in August, our third child, Dee, was born. With me away from Second Street and the bedbug invasion a recent memory, Paul and the others were delighted when Mrs. O'Brien came to clean the rectory. Her husband, a city sanitation worker, had been killed shortly before in a fall from his truck when he was drunk. She came to our house to beg, and Kim gave her some food and a loan for back rent. She insisted on cleaning our house to work off the money, and then stayed on. One eye was disfigured and had almost no vision, her gray hair was thin, her face was worn and too lined for her fifty-odd years, but her spirit was indefatigable. By the time I got back to the house with Dee, after a month with Paul's family in the country, she was firmly wedded to "the fathers" (she always spoke of them collectively). She was also attached to my white monogrammed wash cloths—remembrance of things past—with which she was washing soot off the window sills when I walked in with the baby. I stiffened when Mrs. O'Brien, about whom I had only heard, rushed to greet me, and attempted, with loud clucking noises, to shift the baby from my arms to hers. I alone would carry my baby to the bedroom. Still cooing, she chucked mother and daughter under the chin, escorted us upstairs and stood, monogrammed wash cloth in hand, watching me settle the baby in the crib in our room. Mrs. O'Brien had come into the house as a protectress for her priests, and she wasn't sure I belonged.

"I been taking care of them since you been gone," she said, sidling up to the crib.

"Everything seems fine," I answered without conviction, eyeing the shapeless figure in the flowered housedress over a man's well-worn shirt, its unbuttoned cuffs hanging loosely on her red wrists. On her feet she wore shabby felt slippers as gray and wispy as her hair, and her stockings were heavy and brown even in warm September. Her apron was dark with a bibbed front, the kind cobblers wear. It was tied at hip level, and she stood with her left hand tucked in its knotted belt, her right hand making ineffective swipes at the crib with my wash cloth. Five o'clock came and she left with a final "kitchy koo" at the sleeping infant.

Mrs. O'Brien stayed with us for three years, after having come to give a couple of days' work in return for a loan. Much of this time was spent leaning on her broom watching her beloved fathers eat, or pouring their coffee with her gnarled, lumpy hands and adoringly setting down the cups with a great clatter. The greater part of the day she spent sweeping each room with lingering strokes that eventually pushed piles of dust to the center of the floor, where nine times out of ten they would remain. From the very beginning she dismissed the vacuum cleaner as far too complicated.

Her affectionate nature and tireless good spirits were reserved for my male colleagues; I remained an oddity, to be observed but never clasped to the same bosom. A couple of times a week she would catch me when my nerves were somewhat frayed, stand six inches away from me and ask with shrill sympathy, "Tired, lady?"

I wanted to choke her, but I managed a shrug or an unconvincing "Oh, no."

With her special fortitude, Mrs. O'Brien nonetheless endured the din and traffic of those early years. She considered herself protector of the clergy and the house, but her welcome was forthcoming for anyone, even Dennis and his friends ringing the bell for a glass of water.

It was late September, just short of three months since we had followed the van through the Holland Tunnel and been greeted by the dying dog and the "Keep Out" sign. Our two older children, still too young for school, were content with the confines of the yard and sidewalk. We had lost their F.A.O. Schwartz sandbox to the cats, and its bright-colored panels found an ignominious end in our battered trash cans.

The baby slept in her carriage, where I could watch her from my kitchen window.

The kitchen had become more and more the center of our life. In the early morning when I fed the children, the sun poured in. "Make a yellow room," the children would beg, and I would pull down the shades on the still curtainless windows. Softened by the shades, the morning light yellowed the white enamel of the refrigerator and the stove, and the children were content. Often Dennis would stop by on his way to school. He became a breakfast visitor. Often Mae and Frank came, eager for coffee. They were more tense now that their four children were in school. Without the buffer of their offspring, they argued with each other constantly and yet with resignation.

Disregarding me and the children as we ate, they would review in querulous antiphony the death of their fourteen-year-old Davie, as if somehow only that nagging tragedy prevented them from being happy, employed, and secure. When it was over, Mae would hunt for a kleenex in her purse, snapping it open and shut in staccato, and Frank soften and put his arm around her shoulders. "You're always right. You go home now and leave me to talk to the fathers about a job. They're hiring again at Western Electric."

Some mornings when Frank was working, Mae came alone. She was still preoccupied with thoughts of Davie, but these times she would speak of him at Christmas or Easter or tell us about his first day at school, as if he weren't dead at all, as if when Frank weren't there she could not bring herself to admit that finality.

There were weeks when we saw neither of them, except Frank briefly when he worked at the church on Saturday. Mae would be working in a local factory or as a salesgirl, "helping Frank out," she explained. "Davie hated me to work. 'Wait till I'm raised, Mom,' he used to say, 'and I'll give you every little thing you need.' "

All our days were filled with callers. It was then a telephone-less neighborhood, and people came to ask help in finding jobs, to talk over troubles with their landlords, to have Paul, Kim, or Bob go with them to court. The clerical collar accompanying someone to court made a difference, especially for a Negro. If a priest came in with a boy who had been picked up for stealing, for instance, the judge would often turn to the priest to ask about the boy's family or the circumstances of the arrest. Those underage were either sent to a county juvenile center, or roundly scolded, or put in the custody of the church—a rather informal situation which meant we kept in touch with the boy for a while.

At about this time we began an uneasy alliance with the Jersey City police. They began to rely on us for help with children who needed the recreation Grace Church provided, and to help evicted families find housing when no agency would. Yet they resented us for complicating their beat on Second Street with crowds of children and teen-agers leaving the parish hall after an evening of television, crafts, or basketball. In turn, the police angered us with their lack of interest in the causes of crime, their rough treatment of mere suspects, the name calling and rubber-hose tactics, but we had to depend on them. We called them when drunks passed out in the church or at the lych-gate and couldn't be prodded into motion. We called them when money or church and office equipment were stolen.

An amateur psychologist once wryly said, "When kids begin to steal, you know they love you." By that standard, devotion was deeply rooted after a year. Our youthful visitors had lost their awe of our house and reluctance to enter it. They came, they saw, and often they took. The thefts were almost always committed by teen-age boys, Negro and white. What they took over the years ranged from a handful of change on a dresser, to keys for the rectory and the church, to typewriters. On a couple of occasions, the Sunday collection was removed from the safe, left unlocked by mistake. The police eventually retrieved large objects like typewriters from pawnshops, and sometimes the money was replaced. But we began locking the church in mid-evening and the rectory when we were upstairs and the first floor left untended. We kept a sharper watch on rectory gatherings when kids were around, and no one was allowed upstairs unless invited. We had found that our theories of a wide-open church and rectory needed limits.

Dealing with thievery was always painful: the pit-of-the-stomach reaction when something was gone, the ordeal of accusing the culprit, the conflict we felt, since no matter what the accused had taken we had more, which obscured the simple fact that he was a thief, and the discomfort of feeling we'd been an easy mark.

With time, dirt, successions of people, problems of discipline, and fatigue, tensions mounted within our household. "You can't expect to be happy all the time," Paul tried to say to me soothingly after a memorable explosion on my part. I screamed through tears of rage that I wasn't two years old. Bob and Kim heard the exchange, and their laughter floated back to me through an angry haze. That morning a rat had jumped off my washing machine. I can still hear the thud of his body and feel the tail whipping my legs as he raced by. But there was more than early morning rats. Four very different personalities were under one roof.

Kim was extreme. He sensed drama in every encounter. When Naomi finally walked across our threshold, he felt that it was one more blow against the foe (greed, discrimination, or the image of the Episcopal Church as caring only for the rich). Personal comfort meant little to him, and he always thought of concepts like Welcome and Succor in the most absolute terms. While sharing the same concerns as Kim, and to the same degree, Bob was more conservative. He wanted to help each individual, in whose dignity he deeply believed, but he also wanted time to be alone. He would have liked more privacy in our house.

While still in New York, we had worked out some of the details of living together. The plan was that Kim and Bob would fix breakfast in the parish hall, the three men would eat lunch out to discuss the problems of the day, and we would all eat dinner together. As for drinking, we would limit ourselves primarily to beer.

Once we had arrived, there had to be a decision about our community meal. Bob said it was a Moore household, that whether we ate in the dining room or not was my affair. Kim insisted we were in kitchen-table land and it was important that we break down this simple barrier and eat where we presumed lower Jersey City ate—in the kitchen. We agreed with Kim but without his passion. By fall, the white enamel table was set with forks and spoons and plastic ware, the silver and wedding presents put away.

Democracy did not always work smoothly within the rectory community. Kim and Bob couldn't understand why we needed plans (or at least so many of them) for our family existence, and Paul and I remarked in private conversations about the vagueness of bachelors. We disagreed over discipline, whether it was coping with Dennis running to the third floor without permission, Horatio throwing bags of water off the fire escape, or one of the older boys caught in a theft. Kim was the most lenient, Bob tended to be strict, and Paul and I stood somewhere in the middle. We never really agreed—each person simply acted as he felt he should in each situation. It was our way of reconciling individual differences, or at least of not confronting them head on, and usually it worked well enough, although it had its drawbacks, particularly when some joint action was necessary.

By fall we had learned to be strict with each other about time off. A devoted friend came over from the Bronx one day each week, cared for the children and cooked so that

Paul and I could go together to his mother's apartment in New York. Kim and Bob each took a day. The four of us grew sensitive to each other's breaking points. Kim had great endurance, but there were times when he would grow impenetrably silent, descend to the basement, and sit in one of the damp rooms on the swivel chair that didn't work. There he would stay for perhaps an hour, arms at his side, feet stretched out on another chair, with his black fedora pulled down over his face. Bob took things more slowly, but finally, when he had listened patiently to too many peoples' problems, tried with twenty interruptions to write a sermon, and reprimanded endless little boys for being noisy in our front yard, his step could be heard as he slowly climbed the two flights of stairs to his room, where with unmistakable finality he would close the door.

Fortunately, none of us traveled these escape routes simultaneously. Even Paul and I were frantic at different moments. Paul had a slow, steady ascent to boiling. He would become more and more conscientious, the furrows on his forehead would deepen, the jaw would set firmly. The explosion was marked by a compulsion to straighten up his bureau. The only abnormal part of this operation was that it took at least fifteen minutes to complete, and a good deal of arm-swinging was involved. I pursued a more uneven course: irritation when too many people asked me where someone else was or when the children and our new baby were kept awake by front yard departures and arrivals, noisier exasperation after Mrs. O'Brien's query, "Tired, lady?" and, finally, mock calm and paranoid silence. My temper would then wear itself out in a hyperactive attack on the white woodwork, where finger marks and industrial soot stubbornly remained, despite my scrubbing. We all were aware of the danger signs in each other, and there was much predicting among us of impending emotional storms, always funny unless one's own mood was under analysis.

It was an odd setup—two bachelors in their mid-thirties, a younger married couple with two young children and a new baby, all in what was fast becoming a community center—but the reasons we were there and the deep involvement we felt somehow overshadowed all the little difficulties. Also—slowly—each day's events had become more predictable. We were less shattered by destitution as it became more familiar. The rejected, the hungry, the drunks, the whores, the fools, the exploiters of poverty, the has-beens were no longer strangers.

IX *Second-best China*

"I can't say as I'm crazy about the coloreds, but they're here to stay," Mrs. Powell told us, "and if you don't get 'em together with the likes of Catherine and Sally Hogan, you'll have two churches on your hands." On one of her kitchen visitations, she had persuaded us with this line of thinking that a regular ladies' meeting was the only way to introduce some of the old guard to Mrs. Smith and Mrs. Trotter, Dennis's and Naomi's mothers, whose only contacts with the church were through their children and television. A churchwomen's group still survived, although death, inertia, and the move to the suburbs had removed all but a half-dozen faithfuls. These remaining members had all known Canon Bryan, a symbol, it seemed, of the way things used to be. Implicit in their nostalgia was the suspicion that Grace Church would never have the prestige to attract such a man again. There was hardly a time that Catherine Hogan didn't speak of him to us. "He was handsome—not as tall as you, Father," she told Paul. "He walked everywhere with a large dog on a lead, and he wore a black cape. They knew him at City Hall. He was always down there getting help for one of his flock. Grace Church was his life, Father."

Mrs. Powell wasn't quite so sure. "You don't spend time at City Hall just doing favors for others—that's storybook stuff. As Willie used to say, them Episcopalian round-collars may not line their pockets with dollar bills, but they sure as hell like to be in favor with the higher-ups. And Willie wasn't referrin' to the higher-ups in heaven. He meant downtown."

But even she agreed that the Canon had played a big part in their lives. He had baptized their children; buried their husbands; in some instances, and to their undying shame, he had, with mysterious funds at his disposal, and secretly, of course, tided them over "bad times." After he died, Mrs. Hogan told us that she felt she had spoken for all the living when she had said, "A little of me died, too." She had been president of the Women's Guild for seventeen years, stepping down only when her niece, Sally, reached a suitable age and took over, as Mrs. Hogan succinctly put it, "complete and total responsibility."

Sally, in her late twenties, pushed herself unmercifully. She held down a demanding secretarial job, cleaned her aunt's four-story house—half of it rented out to boarders—and waited on Mrs. Hogan's every need, culinary and conversational. Her aunt, generous as she was with recipes and anecdotes about the Democrats, never let Sally forget that she was an orphan. "Orphaned, but she knows the meaning of duty," she would say. Sally had lived with her since early childhood. When I visited Mrs. Hogan at her house, she led me to the little attic in the eaves and pointed to the small black leather trunk standing in the stale dust. "Sally's hope chest, but I know she'll never use it," she confided.

Sally always smiled when her aunt spoke of her, but the smile seemed to belong more to the faint frown of the brow than to her dimpled mouth. Her shoulders were very wide and hunched slightly forward. She always wore a pastel dress, tight around the upper arms and shiny from many ironings.

For years now, Mrs. Hogan and Sally had planned the fund-raising card parties and bake sales each fall and spring, with some support from Winifred Powell and two or three other parishioners. Catherine Hogan could never bring herself to admit that attendance at these functions had dwindled over the years. Sally told us in private that the last few times the "crowd" had consisted of only a few curiosity seekers who, seeing her hand-painted sign over the parish hall—"Bridge! Pinochle! Door Prizes for All! Cakes and Cookies!"—had wondered if it weren't all free. Verbally at least, Sally could go along with most of what her aunt did on these occasions, but one card party she described for us seemed to offend even her enslaved sensibilities. Four women had wandered in, and, when almost forcibly put at a card table by Mrs. Hogan, they announced in unison that they were "just looking around" and had no money at all, not even change. She let them play one round of auction bridge and said, as Sally quoted her, "What else could I do on church property?" When they left, she whispered to Sally to give each of the two winners a glass ashtray as a door prize and to urge them to come back.

Mrs. Hogan agreed with Winifred Powell: the "new people" should be invited to join the Women's Guild. Privately she told us that she thought two colored members were enough in a group of eight—at least until "they know the ropes." Then she figured ahead a little and could hardly contain herself: "I've always heard they bake grand—hot rolls and fried bread—think of the bake sales, Sally." Sally nodded.

Only days after these preparatory conversations, the first meeting of the new and the old was under way in our living room. The Trotter-Smith contingent had arrived late that evening and sat together near the door on folding wooden chairs. Dennis, perched on the fire escape, greeted his mother through the open window. "Hush," Mrs. Smith said nervously.

Kim introduced the new arrivals. Mrs. Hogan made a dulcet welcoming speech, remarking on the age of the Guild, how it met every month "except—" she lowered her eyes—"in Lent." Its activities were mainly social, she explained, although Canon Bryan had always opened each meeting with prayer and Mr. Everson had continued that custom. When the formal part of her welcome was over and she had responded to the Negro visitors' nods and smiles with nods and smiles of her own, she saw fit to dwell a bit more on Canon Bryan. "He knew everyone in town—politicians, priests, everyone."

"Yep, Bryan was always palling around with the monsignors, all right," Winifred Powell interrupted, her voice rising ominously. "And them Catholic priests know the ballot count as well as the politicians." She pounded her cane on the parquet floor. "It ain't how the ballots go into the box in this town's elections, Catherine Hogan, it's how they come out."

Catherine Hogan was too busy to react, smoothing her skirt and giving Sally loud whispered instructions about taking the new ladies' addresses, so Mrs. Powell challenged her again.

"You heard me, Catherine. They count three ballots for one, flush a bunch down the toilet, or whatever suits them for the final tally."

A Democrat all her life, the widow of one of Mayor Hague's political henchmen, Catherine Hogan could not suffer this kind of attack. She turned toward Mrs. Powell, her dark luminous eyes riveting her with their hooded gaze long before she spoke. She leaned forward. "Winifred Powell, my Ed—God rest his soul—" she paused between words with pious deliberation—"saw to it there was no monkey business on Election Day. He served his city when you and your Willie were down on Erie Street makin' rugs and dreamin' of Herbert Hoover. Him and his chicken in every pot! Why, people were dying on street corners, if they weren't selling apples. We Democrats care—a fine hospital—and the Church —is behind us."

"What church?" snickered Mrs. Powell, bitter with the nagging paranoia that came from being an Episcopalian Republican in Mayor Hague's Catholic, Democratic citadel.

Mrs. Hogan was furious. She, in turn, was sensitive about having married a Roman Catholic, but rather than show her anger she hung her head in simulated grief. "Father here knows how fine Ed was from all those letters he wrote Canon Bryan. The Canon stored them in his study. Ed cared for this church, even if he didn't belong to it. Father, he cared a lot more than Willie Powell."

Mrs. Powell snorted and whacked the arm of the sofa with her knuckles. "They were all crooks, and Ed Hogan was no better than the rest of them."

Mrs. Smith and Mrs. Trotter smiled bravely throughout the exchange but were obviously ill at ease. I didn't know then any of the background of the spat, but I did wonder as I listened if the Salvation Army trucks had carried off any of Canon Bryan's treasured letters from Ed Hogan when we had loaded them with so many cartons of ancient papers and periodicals.

Kim rose from the sofa where he had been sitting and said with a forced smile, "We believe in the two-party system. We believe in Dissent."

"One of them newfangled words of his again," mumbled Mrs. Powell.

Kim laughed and cleared his throat. "A political discussion will have to wait. What we want to talk to you about is Father Moore's ordination. Right after graduation from seminary, in the Episcopal church and in the Roman, too—" he nodded at Mrs. Hogan—"a young man is first ordained to what is known as the diaconate, and six months afterwards to the priesthood. Normally the young deacons go to our cathedral in Newark for this ceremony, but the Bishop really wants to put us on the map, so he plans to have it here. All you ladies will have to give the reception afterwards." Kim had a gift for convincing people of their importance. Whatever he was talking about was of the deepest concern to him, and he conveyed this to everyone.

Mrs. Hogan was the first to speak. Her voice was low and serious, and she leaned forward. "The Guild" (she pronounced it as though it rhymed with "wild") "can do it, Father."

"In our different ways," said Kim, "we are all part of the parish." He nodded at Mrs. Smith near the doorway. "Some of our new friends, whose children are already part of the daily scene—"

"I'll say they are," broke in Mrs. Powell. Mrs. Smith looked embarrassed.

"—will help, I'm sure," Kim continued. "As will Mrs. Powell, because she has been a faithful member for so many years, and you, Mrs. Hogan, because of your long association here and the devoted service you and your niece have given." Sally looked pleased. "Sally is a part of the accomplished choir Mr. Everson left us, and is a comfort to her aunt, Mrs. Hogan," Kim explained for the benefit of the newcomers. Sally glanced at her aunt, as if for permission, and said quietly that she would help with the reception. Mrs. Smith added that she thought so much of Father Moore she would be glad to contribute what time she had. Mrs. Trotter agreed in monosyllables.

Mrs. Hogan plunged on, directing her remarks to Kim. "The china hasn't been used for years—Sally can wash it. We'll make chicken salad—a favorite recipe of Mrs. Hague's." She paused as if to pound home the fact that only she in the group was privy to the secrets of Mrs. Hague's kitchen. "It takes lots of chopped nuts and olives. We'll go to my butcher for the chickens."

All of a sudden Mrs. Powell was on her feet. She steadied the lavender hat on her head and took a deep breath. "Who, Catherine Hogan, died and made you boss?"

The confrontation was brief. Mrs. Hogan fixed her assailant with another of her piercing looks. "Winifred used to go to the same butcher when she and Willie were on Erie Street. He has the best cuts of meat downtown. Did you change to the A & P, Winifred?"

"Howdy's delicatessen's good enough for the likes of me, Madam High-and-Mighty," Mrs. Powell retorted.

"We'll have a couple of months to plan and to work up some committees," said Kim, attempting to avert another argument.

Mrs. Powell was still glum. "I hope that bishop knows what he's doing—ordinating, or whatever the word is. I don't see how you'll have more than fifty people in that great big church, and it'll be winter, too."

"Well, I know you'll all help," said Kim quickly. "Shall we close the meeting with prayer?" Everyone rose, heads bowed.

I stood in the arched doorway near the newcomers, and, as Kim prayed, I realized how uneasy I felt at this confrontation of the two groups, black and white, which, in the normal course of Jersey City social life, would never encounter one another. I realized that we couldn't strip the church of all Mrs. Hogan babbled about—the bazaars, the meetings, the fuss and feathers—and I wanted that church for her in her lonely days, with the petty elegances upon which she depended and whose sham sustained her. But the church of meetings and sewing circles, pretty hats and squabbles wasn't what I wanted for Naomi and Dennis. I wanted it to offer something new for them and for their mothers, who stood silent in my living room surrounded by the institutional church at its least appealing. I wanted Dennis to know that the love of Christ could care for him, that it was stronger than the policeman's rubber hose; I wanted Naomi to know that the church's embrace was stronger than Mr. Felipe's greedy arms. But more important, they must learn that Christ could sustain them in their troubles, that He cared about the run-down houses and the no-breakfasts and the teacher who didn't know how to understand. Elizabethan prayers weren't going to do the trick.

The new and the old were in conflict inside me, too. I was attached to the old values: an orderly house, privacy with my husband, quiet for my family. But, almost despite myself, they faded in importance as my new life grew more compelling. I liked the walks up Mrs. Smith's dark stairs with my children, the glasses of sherry with Mrs. Powell, Naomi's confidences, Dennis's sharing of secret worries, the interminable conversations with people about their problems.

My reverie was terminated abruptly by a sharp jab in the ribs from Mrs. Powell. "Ain't it gettin' cold up there in the clouds? Come on down with the rest of us where it's warm."

I laughed and walked her to the door. "I hope you'll help with the ordination reception," I said as she jammed the long hairpin securing her straw hat into what seemed to be the center of her skull.

"We'll see if General Hogan in there can give me some real big job—like takin' pits out of them olives she makes such a fuss about. Yes, I'll help." She marched out to the sidewalk.

Mrs. Smith and Mrs. Trotter left next. They thanked me for the evening and assured Mrs. Hogan they would help with the ordination festivities. They had said almost nothing during the meeting, and their smiles seemed forced as they walked out the door. I wondered if they'd come back.

Mrs. Hogan and Sally stood in the front hall long after everyone else had gone. I sat on the stairs, and Kim had his hand on the door, which he had started to pull open for our remaining guests. We were joined by Bob and Paul.

"Father Pegman—" Mrs. Hogan had great difficulty with Bob Pegram's last name—"Sally and I are going to prepare chicken salad—Mrs. Hague's recipe—Ed got it for me one election year—for Father Moore's ordination. The ladies are putting on an affair after the service."

"That'll be just fine, Mrs. Hogan. It'll be lovely, I imagine." Bob's Southern manners came to the fore. "I hope all the ladies will have a part in it," he added.

"Father Myers says we'll have committees. Sally's going to wash up the church china we haven't used for years. Maybe Mrs. Moore could borrow some silver coffee urns from one of the, uh, better churches on the Hill." I said I would try and hoped I could help, too. "No," she said firmly, "it's your day—yours and Father Moore's. Father Pegman says it will be lovely." She started to leave.

"I like the new colored women," she said from the doorway. "I'd like to have them over for tea someday. We'll use the second-best china." I glanced quickly at Paul. It was hard to believe we had heard right, but it was a refrain she was to repeat often.

We walked them to the gate. No one was around. Dennis had deserted the fire escape ladder, from which he had watched the beginning of the meeting.

Mrs. Hogan turned to speak to Paul under the streetlight. "I said to Sally coming over here, Father, that the Bishop is going to be laying his hands on a big overgrown kid when he ordains you."

This had been Paul's first meeting with Catherine Hogan, and he was not about to crumple under her patronizing appraisal. He said good night abruptly, and she fixed him with a look brimming with so many attempted virtues that they seemed to cancel each other out. "Pray for me, Father. You know I'll pray for you—and wait till you taste my chicken salad," she said.

"It sounds great," Paul said, his composure regained, and the Hogans walked off.

The street was quiet and empty save for a drunk asleep in a doorway. He lay on his stomach, and his body above the waist was inside the dark hall. Only his feet and the backs of his legs were visible, twitching in the glow of the streetlight. His heels were turned out, and the toes of the dusty shoes made an awkward V.

Paul and Bob went over to him, and I returned to the house. Minutes later I saw them from the window of our bedroom, Bob and Paul supporting the man and making shuffling progress up the walk. It was both funny and pitiful, the moonlight setting in relief the three incongruous figures moving across the concrete—one step forward, shift for balance, forward again. I went downstairs to let them in.

At our kitchen table the man wept, denied that he ever drank, gulped coffee, and was alternately silent and verbose. His name was Wolowski, and he was of Polish extraction. "And you, Father, appear to be of Polish extract as well," he said, pointing a wobbly finger at Bob's bald head. "My whole family lose their hair just like you."

"No," said Bob with what we, shaking with laughter, felt was unnecessary firmness. "My family was English. We've lived in Virginia for generations."

Mr. Wolowski waved his hands in front of his face as if clearing away a thick fog. "What you doing at a nigger church, then? I don't associate with them myself."

There was no point in arguing with him. Instead, we told him it was time to leave. He knew far more about possible places to sleep than we did. There was no place he could sleep for free, and there were no fifty cent flops in Jersey City as in the Bowery; the cheapest room was $1.50 a night. We gave him the money, and he swept, courtierlike, from our kitchen, swearing undying devotion. In the morning we found him again, lying against the church doorway, blood dried on his cheek, a new bottle propped between his knees. All we did was wake him, feed him more coffee, and ask him to move along.

In all our years with the Mr. Wolowskis of this world, we never resolved the dilemma of what to do about the men who came shivering to our door in shirt sleeves but who would probably hock the secondhand jacket from our basement clothes room for wine, and drink up the money intended for a night's lodging in the flop house.

x *The Laying On of Hands*

Our first and most permanent bequest from the police was Harry, who came to our door one day at their suggestion—and never left. Captain Deenan of the local precinct telephoned first and told Paul that Harry McAllister had gone to the public baths to clean up and had our address in his pocket.

"He got sick when the circus left town and used his last dime, he says, to travel out here by subway to find some nephew. Now no nephew, no place to live. You don't know what's cock-and-bull and what ain't. We got no place to send him, no way to find a job for an old guy. See what you can do for him."

My first view of Harry was through the small panes of the storm door. Clad in baggy pants and jacket, he was lifting his feet in a sort of soft-shoe routine without moving to left or right. I could see his square ruddy face under the crown of the military-style cap. He waved at me through the glass, bending closer, and I caught sight of very blue eyes smiling at me. I kept expecting him to speak, but when none of my three hellos was answered other than by a hand raised to the shiny black visor in an extended salute, I pushed open the door. I suppose that in a way he was a clown, although his career with Mr. Barnum, from what the police had learned, appeared to have been one of maintenance. He stood like a clown, once the shuffling dance step subsided, with feet turned slightly out, arms held stiff and away from his body, and the classic clown smile set tightly in a thin curve. I urged him in.

He sat at the kitchen table gulping coffee and tearing hunks of bread off an unsliced loaf, and told me about behind-the-scenes life under the big top. He puffed with pride when reporting to me that Roy Rogers's act was with the circus for the season. "Trigger whinnies when he hears my voice. Roy and Dale wouldn't let no one else touch him. Roy is a good friend of mine." Then he was downcast. "But I got sick—they left without me—what's that horse going to do? And them elephants?" Harry wailed.

I tried to assure him that someone else must be able to care for his charges, but that only intensified his grief. All his moods, I soon learned, were extreme but brief. After a moment he raised his head from the table where he had been cradling it on his outstretched arms. The blue eyes looked up, their expression ultraserious. "Roy will find a way—and them elephants can manage." I agreed that somehow the show would go on. He heaved his shoulders in resignation and rallied.

"Your yard needs sweeping." Within minutes he was at work with the push broom up and down the front walk. When he had fussed over the twenty-minute job for an hour, he was back in the kitchen holding the broom at attention as if it were a musket. My praise not coming quickly enough to suit him, he rapped the broom handle on the floor.

"Well?"

"Good job, Harry. It certainly needed it."

Paul took over after the sweeping was completed and found Harry a cheap room in a neighborhood boardinghouse. Harry was very proud and produced a worn twenty-dollar bill from his pocket. "I suppose—" a little more soft-shoe motion as he spoke—"you think Mr. Barnum and Mr. Bailey didn't treat me right. I took charity from the hospital, but no more, Father. That's the God's truth."

He was back the next day for another sandwich and cup of coffee and insisted on sweeping the same walk. For the first few months he ate dinner with us every day. Later he came for Sunday and holiday dinners and wangled other evening meals for half price in a local diner. He continued the sweeping and ran errands for us in exchange for a tiny weekly salary.

Harry was settled in by the time the last feverish preparations were underway for Paul's ordination. Sally Hogan, Mrs. Hyde, who had been brought into the woman's guild, and others scrubbed the kitchen in the parish hall, and Mrs. Hogan personally escorted her butcher over with the much-touted chicken.

"The cost may be more, but the supermarket chickens are frozen too long," Mrs. Hogan declared as she stacked the parcels of meat in the old-fashioned ice box. "Real risky, Mr. Peck says. Don't you, Mr. Peck?" He nodded affably, wiping his hands on a soiled patch of his white butcher's apron.

"Mr. Peck knows the people who pluck his chickens," continued Mrs. Hogan. "Ed, God rest his soul—" the eyes were suddenly lowered so that only the heavy dark lids were visible—"used to say—" eyes lifted and luminous again—"he was glad there was something left like the old days. Don't ever change, George. Ed called you George, didn't he?"

"Yes, ma'am. He was a fine man, your husband." He bowed to Mrs. Hogan. "Ma'am, I left my shop alone. Nice to meet you folks." He bowed again and left.

Mrs. Hyde and Sally gave a whole day to washing the heavy china. Harry swept and swept. The grass was almost all worn away in the little lawn Mrs. Everson had tended so carefully, and the day before the ordination Harry swept the packed-down dirt. "Make it real flat—things gotta be just perfect," he explained. His sweeping was a Chaplinesque performance with a repeating cycle. First, he would lean hard on his push broom, heavy body set with one foot forward, staring off into space like the sea captain two doors down. Then, as if he had been wound up like a toy, he would fling himself into frenzied sweeping before running down and finally standing quiet again, admiring his handiwork and observing the world.

Harry's coming into our midst with such confidence right before the celebration for Paul piqued Mrs. O'Brien. She felt he was making uncalled-for inroads on her domain. He called me "Mommy" from the first and had a proprietary attitude toward the property. Both intimacies irked her. She tried to make a joke of his feelings.

The day before the ordination, she stood on the rectory stoop, her broom propped up next to the front door, while Harry swept the yard with a carefully worked out circular pattern in mind. Whenever he rounded the curve nearest the door, she would cup her mouth with both hands and let him have it:

"Harry'd give more than fifty cents
To see the elephant jump the fence."

I watched the scene from the kitchen window. Purple in the face, Harry finished his project, swept the trash onto a folded section of newspaper, and stormed into the kitchen. He stood in the corner holding the trash in front of him.

"I mean it—you know how it is, Mommy—she's gonna get it. There I was cleaning up the yard for Father's whatchacall-it tomorrow, and she's out there singing some damn fool song." I calmed him as best I could, but he and Mrs. O'Brien were red-faced and silent in each other's presence for weeks afterwards.

The ordination was on a Saturday morning in December.

It was the first visit for many of our relatives and old friends. Harry was finishing a cup of coffee when the doorbell started ringing. Dennis and his friends answered the door and escorted guests proudly into our already crowded kitchen.

It was a raw day, but Mrs. Powell stood on the corner of the church block during the time guests were arriving. Quite unsolicited, she assumed a tour-guide role, combining church information with a bit of autobiographical material. "I've been around seventy-one years, and the church's stood here a quarter of a century longer" was her opening gambit. When one visitor asked her to identify the local Catholic church, she drew herself up to her full five feet. "That," she replied grandly, pointing at St. Mary's across the street, "is the Roman Catholic church, and this—" she paused, pivoted on her heel, and tapped Grace Church's iron fence with her cane—"is the Holy Catholic Church."

Paul's parents came. Mrs. Moore went upstairs to help get her grandchildren ready. Mr. Moore, an elderly businessman, silently wondering why his grandchildren lived in such confusion, shook hands with anyone whose hand he could reach, as though he were at a Board of Directors meeting, and went into the living room just in time to see Mrs. O'Brien sweep a small pile of dirt under the rug. He sat there in relative peace while people swirled in and around the front hall and kitchen. Honor, then four, decided it would be a good moment to show her grandfather her baby turtle, a recent birthday present, and even more fun to remove it from its shallow dish and carry it to him on a saucer. Mr. Moore, intent on accepting anyone or anything presented to him on his visit to Second Street, reached out for what he thought was a midmorning cracker. Only a scream from his granddaughter saved him from plunging the tiny animal, shell and all, down his throat.

While this commotion was going on in the living room, I was with Mrs. Moore and the other two children, trying to empty the house for the service. We finally left the house, only to find more commotion on the street with the arrival of still another Moore generation, Paul's ninety-year-old grandmother in her maroon Rolls Royce. Dennis and his friends were first mesmerized by the car, then overcome with boyish curiosity. They didn't wait for Granny to emerge before exploring its recesses. I decided not to get involved in their extrication, and Granny politely identified the car's interior furnishings for the three little boys, finally stepping out with them stumbling along behind her. Embarrassed by such a symbol of opulence at our crumbling curb, I decided to ignore the car and simply explained to Mrs. Hogan and Sally that a driver was needed to take care of Mrs. Moore in her old age. "I went out to greet them," Mrs. Hogan replied, "and he said he'd been in her employ for forty years."

But it was a wonderful day. Grace Church was filled with members who had moved and come back for the occasion, with the new people that now called it home, with friends and family. Seminary friends made up the choir. Harry stood in the back as serious as a sentinel at the grave of a king. Mrs. O'Brien, in a back pew, was smiling in her sleep. Mrs. Powell made a late entrance, stopping every six feet or so on her way up the center aisle to survey the people before finally plumping herself down under the pulpit. Mrs. Smith and Mrs. Trotter watched from a pew as Dennis and Horatio, dressed as altar boys for the first time, flanked the Bishop at the start of the service.

At first, I found myself more aware of my small children riffling through the pages of prayer books than of the ceremony at the altar. I heard a baby crying and noises from the street. Around me I was aware both of the fur coats and of the clothes from the Salvation Army, of polished mahogany as well as of places on the wall where the paint was peeling. Almost dully I listened to the prayers of the Bishop. I wondered what Paul was thinking. It was difficult for me to see his kneeling figure. And then those dramatic words, and I had to listen. "Receive the Holy Ghost for the office and work of a priest in the Church of God"—the Bishop and all the priests present reached forward and placed their hands on Paul's head—"now committed unto thee by the imposition of our hands." The Bishop went on: "Whose sins thou dost forgive, they are forgiven . . ." and I thought of the sins among us—the hidden ones, the obvious ones. And I was moved.

At the end of the service, we went up to the altar rail for the new priest's blessing. Then it was over. The ceremony was done.

After the service, everyone went to the reception at the parish hall. The Hogan chicken salad was exclaimed over, Paul smiled and shook hands, a picture was taken of four Moore generations. Mrs. Hyde presided over the coffee. Sally Hogan and Mrs. Smith passed the plates of salad. Mae Corey was in charge of cookies (a tiered cake had in the end been voted down as too delicate to handle). People greeted each other. Dennis, chased by Horatio, crawled under a long table. I remember joy and confusion and wondering if I shouldn't suddenly feel noble when I just felt tired.

People began to leave. Paul and I went out on the street for the good-byes. Lucille, huddled in a blanket, was on her stoop watching her little boys on their creaky tricycles. Mr. D'Agostino, driven inside by the December weather, was barely visible reading his paper behind his dirty plate-glass window. We watched him for a minute, but he didn't raise his head. Harry was sweeping again; Dennis and Horatio were throwing a ball against the neighboring wall. Mrs. Powell came out of the hall with the Hogans and Mrs. Hyde.

"We cleaned everything up. Mrs. Hyde and Sally washed every cup, and there's a lot of trash for Harry. Wasn't the chicken good, Father?" Mrs. Hogan lingered, Sally and Mrs. Hyde beside her, smiling.

"Everything was wonderful, Catherine," Paul said.

"And the Bishop was just grand—but did you see those colored kids under the table? And there were so many compliments about the chicken." She talked on and on, Sally nodding in agreement. At long last everyone was gone. Bob and Kim were straightening up the church, our children were napping after all the excitement, and even Dennis went home. A scruffy cat wandered out from behind the garbage can and stretched in the weak afternoon sun. Lucille called her little boys and pushed them, tricycles and all, into the dark hallway. The street was quiet. We walked back to the house, and found Harry sitting in the kitchen.

"I guess they made you a whatcha-call-it now. I'm real proud." He stood and hugged Paul. "But we gotta do something about the grass in front of the church."

He talked on about the grass, but it was hard for us to be interested. Finally, he rose to go, turning to me when he reached the door. "When the circus comes back, Mommy, we'll hire a truck and back the elephant right up to the gate. It's the best manure that is, Mommy."

XI The Time the Reindeer Died

It was already the day of the church Christmas party when Harry found out that a fancy costume for Santa wasn't in the budget. First he was silent, his mouth set in a hard little line of exasperation. Then he tugged indignantly at his lapels, and pulled his cap with its full tweedy crown and shiny visor lower over his brow to cushion the expected rebuff. "Gotta rent the suit, Mommy—beard's gotta be real hair."

"Harry, we'll make one. It'll be just as good," I said, and sent Dennis off to buy red crepe paper and pins at the local Woolworth's.

"Now looky here. The fathers want me to give the kids a real good time. You wreckin' things again, Mommy. It ain't fair to no one, and you know dang well," he whined.

He had calmed down somewhat by the time Dennis returned, and we trooped up to my bedroom for the fitting. Mrs. O'Brien appeared in the doorway, full of suggestions for cutting out the suit. She insisted on helping me lay out strips of paper on the bed. Honor came in.

"What's it going to be, Mommy?" she said as Harry made a sputtering noise.

"Santy Claus is going to bring you a dolly if you're real good, and Harry's going to be Santy," Mrs. O'Brien crooned. "Isn't that right, lady?"

"We're making a suit for Harry. Just sometimes you have a dress-up Santa, but soon we'll go to Gimbels and see the *real* Santa Claus." (This was one of my least favorite maternal lies, but it wasn't the time for the final myth-shattering Santa speech.)

"Can we go right now?" asked Honor.

"Let me hold the pins for you," Mrs. O'Brien said, pressing closer.

"Thank you, the pins are fine on the bed," I said, while Honor, pulling at my dress, asked me again when we were going to Gimbels. Harry, meanwhile, was stomping around like a race horse flirting with the starting gate. I pinned the paper over his shoulders and around his neck whenever he was still.

"Too bad Father isn't here to help you." Mrs. O'Brien came close to the bed with her broom and gazed at me.

"We can manage," I said. Honor gathered the pins from the bed in one small hand, then dropped them.

"Father has too much on his mind to help you, huh?" Mrs. O'Brien got down on all fours to pick up the pins. She stuck them between her lips as she collected them, which made all further comments about my costume-making incomprehensible.

"The floor's dirty," said Honor triumphantly, jumping on the bed and holding up the palms of her hands.

"Gotta eat a peck of dirt before you die," Harry cackled, then screamed—"Ouch! You stuck me, Mommy—ouch, ouch!"

"What's a peck, Mommy?" asked Honor.

Harry jumped forward as he yelped, holding his pin-pricked neck. I was pulled along, one end of the roll of crepe paper in my hand, the other attached to Harry. Honor ran up and down on the bed, delighted at the antics. Mrs. O'Brien stood, mouth full of pins, hand outstretched with one for me to use, triumphant that she had gotten into the act.

"Come on, Harry, quiet down. We have to finish up." I pinned frantically.

"Tired, lady?" spat Mrs. O'Brien through the remaining pins.

"There's the doorbell," I said, not sure what I had heard but anxious to reduce the cast of characters. Mrs. O'Brien turned for the stairs, pushing a pile of crepe paper scraps into the corner with her broom as she left. Honor ran off to race her to the front door.

Clutching the unpinned lapels of Harry's red suit, I backed him up to a full-length mirror. He turned around, the sad clown. "The kiddies will know who I am," he complained. I was not aware that we had set our aims as high as complete camouflage.

"Wait till we get the beard done," I said loudly. I wrenched a couple of feet of cotton from its midnight blue wrapper and struggled to pull it into a beard shape. I pinned a fold of red paper around Harry's head and attached it to a long length of cotton. The result looked more like a bee keeper's helmet than St. Nick's stocking cap, but the beard was long and full and that pleased Harry.

By the time we were through with the *haute couture,* the party was underway. I covered Harry with a large overcoat of Paul's and pushed him, head down, over to the parish hall as though we were under fire from sidewalk guerrillas. Children, including ours, were waiting with Paul, Kim, and Bob, impatient for the party to begin. Harry and I waited in the crumbling little vestibule (even the floor had begun to buckle in spots) between the large kitchen and the hall, where we could peek into the auditorium without being seen.

Inside, on the stage, Mrs. Hyde had rigged a wire from which she had hung a couple of old bedspreads to serve as curtains. From my vantage point, I could see Dennis holding nervously to the end of one half of the makeshift curtain and Horatio struggling with the other, preparing to draw it open at the proper moment. In the front row, Mrs. Powell held grimly onto a cowbell borrowed for the occasion. Paul and Bob were walking up and down the rows, trying to calm the kids, and Kim was playing "Jingle Bells" on the piano, accompanying the children's excited voices. Naomi, feeling a shade too old for the party, turned the pages of the music for him. Someone signaled Mrs. Powell, who walked around to the back of the curtain, rang her cowbell with vigor, and returned to her seat.

The curtain pulled back with a screech of metal ring on metal wire. The children clapped wildly, but the stage where Santa was supposed to gambol was empty. Mrs. Powell shook the cowbell again, this time from her chair. The sonorous tones could hardly be described as the jingling associated with Santa, but the audience was not discriminating. The clapping gave way to whispers, then silence throbbing with anticipation.

Harry's mood had completely crumpled when he and I had entered the "wings." Finally I hissed to him that he had to appear, that the children would be upset, that we had all worked so hard. Using all my strength, I began pushing him between his shoulder blades. Slowly and grimly, head lowered, he inched his way to the front of the stage.

After a minute of silence, Bob tried the conversational approach. "Well, Santa, hard to make it without snow?" Silence. Harry's head remained bowed, the cotton beard hanging almost to his waist.

"How's Mrs. Santa?"

"Terrible," Harry replied.

The children began to look at each other. Bob was running out of small talk. "Santa, I'd like to introduce you to Father Moore. He's got a few things to ask you," said Bob, taking a seat with the children as Paul stepped up to the stage.

"Sure, I know Santa," said Paul, too jovially, "and I bet he has a lot of wonderful helpers."

"Nope," Harry grunted, shrugging his shoulders.

Paul tried to cover the growing restlessness of the children with a forced laugh and launched into a new topic. "We'd love to hear about Santa's reindeer. How are all those reindeer feeling after the long trip? How about naming them for him, kids?"

As a few Donders and Blitzens trebled out, Harry raised his head. "They all died," he moaned. Some children giggled without much conviction; a few started crying. Mrs. Hyde rushed up on stage and tried to cheer Santa by placing a limp sack of presents on his lap. He looked up at her.

"You left the toys in the sleigh, Santa," she said, smiling. The children lined up in single file in front of him, and his spirits lightened as he passed out the presents. Kim pounded out another verse of "Jingle Bells"; candy and the toys gave the party a new focus. Harry sat on the stage, red-papered legs dangling, and chuckled at the goings-on. In succeeding years, a real Santa suit rented for the big day kept the reindeer alive and a smile on Harry's face, but he was never a natural for the role.

Harry wasn't the only one who cared about having the right costume. Without something new to wear, we learned, it wasn't really Christmas for the people on Second Street. "I Saw Mommy Do the Mambo With You Know Who" had been booming over the loudspeaker on Newark Avenue titillating crowds of shoppers. In a long list of Christmas ballads it was a low point. With its bumpy rhythms in the background, parents, teen-age unmarried mothers, middle-aged women whose husbands had deserted them, grandmothers taking care of otherwise untended grandchildren, all made down payments on Christmas clothes.

Mae hounded Frank about money. "How do you think

Dolores is going to feel—all those kids with new coats, and her with that one she had so long. Dolores says to me, 'Mamma, why can't I have one with fur?' and I say, 'Girl, you're lucky we got twelve dollars to go on that red one—fur collar or no.' "

"God knows I'm trying, Mae, but everyone needs jobs now. We still gotta eat," answered Frank as though he had said it a hundred times.

We learned about the Christmas problems of the Smith household from Dennis. "We's all gonna get some kinda new clothes if my father don't be laid off. Him and Mamma was really yelling last night, her saying 'Them kids'll all be in rags Christmas,' and Daddy answerin' her quick, 'You think I'm made of money?' "

Each year in early December we could sense the change of mood that came with Christmas. People began to feel uneasy; rent was neglected, and eviction became a real possibility, what with the added burden of payments on the new clothing. The cold became colder, the fuel bills higher; people drank more, feelings were more difficult to handle.

In the world we had left, Christmas had seemed to soften the hard edges of wealth; generosity blossomed briefly. As a child I remember thinking how people I really didn't like suddenly became my best friends at Christmas dinner; stern uncles became benign; even scrambled eggs tasted better on Christmas morning. God was good, and Santa belonged to everyone. When I thought of the poor, I imagined quaint garrets and children's noses pressed longingly against bakery windows. I had pictured them in my mind's eye, but the picture lacked life and feeling. Dennis did not live in a garret but in a tenement, with many others and vicious, real rats and cold and smelly stairwells. For Dennis to have sweets meant going to school with no breakfast, coming home to no dinner.

Now I was in my mid-twenties, and at Christmastime it

seemed as if a great collective frustration were shaking the world. There were fires, thefts, accidents, shootings—more now than during the rest of the year. It was as if the inequities, the unevenness of life, suddenly had become too much. Small luxuries became necessities; what had been bearable, unbearable.

"You care about the coloreds, look at this." Mrs. Powell threw the newspaper on the table as we ate. It was a few days before Christmas. "This is the kind of thing those fancy Democrats don't give a hang about. Voted in by the people—tommy rot!"

A front-page article described a small fire in a basement coal bin early that morning. The bin housed Pearl Lee and her nine children. Soon there was to be a tenth. No one had been injured, but now the family had no place to go. Authorities were investigating the matter, the last paragraph reported. The newspaper account was accompanied by a half-page of pictures. The first one showed Mrs. Lee's home: a daybed, a kerosene lantern, a tiny oil stove for heat (she cooked upstairs on a neighbor's hot plate and carried the food down three flights to her children), an artificial Christmas tree with a few feathery white branches still intact, the rest charred by the fire. The caption read "Lantern is culprit in Yuletide blaze." For the second shot, the photographer had posed the mother on the studio couch as though she were reclining on a boudoir sofa, and had positioned the children around her. Even the smiles he had summoned forth were obscenely convincing. The caption read "Mother-to-be seeks home."

Bob knew the particular neighborhood, so he went over that evening. Mrs. Powell insisted on going with him. They reported that Mrs. Lee was caught in the familiar welfare trap. She could not receive the relief available to indigent families because she had not resided long enough in the city and because she was receiving thirty dollars a month from her estranged husband. The housing project had turned them down because the family was too large.

Bob then approached the Board of Health, and the coal bin was condemned as a "dwelling unsuitable for one adult and nine minors." In any event, the Board's report stated, even before the fire it had not been suitable as a "dwelling unit." Their solution was to arrange placement, as they termed it, for Mrs. Lee and the children in a local medical center over the holidays until suitable rooms could be found. The hospital could take all the family except the teen-age boys. "They ain't been North but two weeks," their mother said.

The next day's paper referred to Grace Church's involvement in the case. It brought us a barrage of calls. One woman telephoned the rectory to say she would like to adopt that cute five-year-old, adding that if it didn't work out she could always send him back to his mother. A reporter from a New York newspaper phoned to arrange an interview with us for a feature story about the case, to run over the period of a week. It had so much human interest, he said. But the lady never called back, the reporter didn't come for the interview, and the calls subsided quickly when the story left the front page.

Part of Mrs. Lee's family moved into the hospital, and the three older Lee boys moved in with us. It was Christmas Eve.

Mrs. Powell never got over her visit to the coal bin with Bob. "She had to haul all them kids upstairs for the toilet and drag water down to drink." She told us over and over about what she had seen—the younger children huddled under a blanket on the sagging daybed, the older ones sitting close to the small stove. She made them her cause and advocated it vigorously to our Second Street neighbors.

"What do you think Episcopals are—do good on Sundays

and steal from the poor the rest of the week, like all the Democrats I know? People's starving a block from here," she snorted to Lucille.

Preparing for that first midnight Mass, I felt a suffocating sense of the burdens I knew people had to bear that Christmas. I woke our children and dressed them for church. Dennis and the Lee boys were waiting in the kitchen. The hospital had ruled that the rest of the Lee family were not to be released, even for Christmas Day, until permanent lodging was found. We had a few minutes before the service began; the two older children played on the stairs, and Dee, dressed in bonnet and coat, waited in her bassinet near the boys. When the doorbell rang, Dennis answered it. "They want coffee," he reported. I heated some and took two cups to the men who had rung. With a shuffling of feet and great effort, they both rose from the porch bench as if hoisted by some unseen, unsteady rope, and pushed the door open for me. I knew them, and we greeted each other by name. Ever since Mr. Wolowski's appearance in the fall, men had come almost every evening for coffee and bread, or sometimes for something warm to wear. All of them were part of the local skid row colony. Their farthest journeys took them, occasionally, to the public bath or, if they had a dime, to New York by subway. I handed each man a cup, and they sat again on the low porch bench.

Clarence was one-eyed and garrulous. "You know, Mrs. Moore, I never touch a drop—you know I always tell the truth. Honest to God, we're sorry to bother you like this—busy with the children, God love them." His face was red, and the flesh around the disfigured eye was livid. I guessed he had pawned his jacket, for he stood in the cold in shirt sleeves, assuring me of his sobriety with teetering aplomb. My gorge rose.

The other one, named George, had an El Greco face, lean

and sad. His hands, fingers stiff from cold, shook so much that the saucer was filled with coffee by the time the cup reached his lips. George's face always disturbed me. You could see to the bottom of it. I had never before understood what the description, "a Christlike face," meant. He started, as if to speak, but I told him I was in a hurry to get over to church with the children. Clarence sat noisily gulping his coffee. I turned to go back in the house. "May I have a match?" George asked. I can still hear the hollow tones. "Asking for a match—I really am the beggar, aren't I, Mrs. Moore?" The pale blue eyes in the gray face looked down at the coffee, and I went back in the house to collect the children. Dennis got him a match for me, and we trooped out. Clarence had fallen asleep, but George rose to admire the baby in my arms as we went through the porch. I asked him to come with us. He said he was not dressed for church.

"Oh, George, it doesn't matter," I told him, but he didn't answer and shuffled off in the moonlit December night, his head hunched down in the thick collar of his jacket. Crossing the street, he made his way against the tide of people streaming toward the high, wide steps of St. Mary's. In the cold vault of the night, holiday voices were sharp and clear. I lost sight of him when he turned the corner. Clarence snored on.

The bell signaling the service at Grace Church gave its final discreet peal, barely audible in the echo of the thunderous gong from St. Mary's, and Dennis, the Lee boys, my children and I walked over to Mass. Lit with candlelight, our church seemed huge. I sat with a woman we had met through friends, a war refugee recently arrived in America. The light flickered on her auburn hair, piled high under a black veil, and there were tears glistening on her cheeks. She knew no one; her son and husband had been killed in Poland. She had come to America to start life again. I caught myself watching her and looked away.

Dennis and the Lees kept dropping hymnbooks from the rack and picking them up. My children played on the pew beside me. Dee dropped her rattle. The scattering of people sang the old Christmas hymns.

Mae and Frank sat with their children in an expressionless row—there were no new clothes. They left the church during one of the carols. Mrs. Powell turned and watched them go. After the service we found Mae in the church vestibule, blood streaming from her wrists. "We have nothing for Christmas," she whispered, "and Davie's gone."

Hardly aware and quite drunk, Frank was slumped outside in the darkness, moaning, "Help me, Father, help me." Their children stood huddled together and silent near the rectory door. Later, Paul, who had taken Mae to the hospital, called to say the wounds weren't serious and she would be well. Frank, who had been waiting for news in our kitchen while he sobered up, went back home with his children. Ours were asleep, and the Lee boys were ensconced on the third floor. It was already Christmas morning.

Each Christmas I see the Lees, grinning around the daybed in that blasphemy of a photograph, and the three boys, who stayed with us until after New Year's, when "suitable rooms" were found. I think of Mae, for whom Christmas thoughts of Davie's death became too much, and of Frank, who couldn't help her. I think of George, the bum, shuffling through the laughing throng of Christmas worshippers. I wonder again if it was a betrayal that we left Jersey City at last. Each Christmas these thoughts crowd, even now, and I push them away.

XII Recognition

A community is a group of people who band together for mutual support because they are stronger together than alone. A Christian community is an open community, offering its warmth to any who wish to come in. As Kim said in his sermon that first Sunday at Grace Church, it is an exchange of love, and the bearing of one another's burdens. In its simplest—and deepest—sense, it is the touch of a hand, laughter, the exchange of names in conversation, the listening to hurts of childhood and age, the sharing of petty worries, the mutual binding, however tenuous, of one another's wounds; it is sheltering, feeding, sharing. It is a joyful place, and it continues because God exists within it, sustaining it.

After our first year in Jersey City, we thought we knew something about community. At that point, we could still use the word without embarrassment, and we spent many hours discussing its meaning for us and for the people who were gathering under the shelter of Grace Church. We also began to accept the fact that things couldn't be changed overnight, and in some cases ever. We had already found that an open-arms approach in the parish would not solve every problem; it was sometimes an invitation to theft instead of trust.

With these thoughts working in our minds, we exported

the children, persuaded a friend from the seminary to take over church and rectory duties, and, tight-lipped and worthy, the four of us charged off for a stock-taking session at a vacation lodge a few hours distant. As we walked in the sunshine and talked, we realized that the problems we had at Grace Church, Jersey City, would be with us as long as we were there. We stepped around them, examining them. We clung to our belief that the difference between a non-Christian and a Christian is that the former may work to alleviate suffering but that the latter attempts to share in it as well. Suffering was part of life, and it had profound meaning for us. We believed that it could be creative, if accepted yet not masochistically sought out, and that sharing it lessened it. We shared insofar as we lived in the midst of it. We laughed, talked, listened, ate, drank, and prayed together with our neighbors. We swept the same dirt, saw the rats, smelled the smells, were antagonistic toward and depended on the same, very human policeman—yet not in the same way. We knew we could afford to eat better than our new friends, take vacations away from the grime, and, finally, enjoy the galling luxury of intellectualizing about life.

We talked of the church building, whose vaulted grandeur had become a symbol of hope to some, but remained alien to others. We talked of church worship—how despite its beauty it seemed so often unrevealing of God's love for all creatures, how by its very inflections it was more comprehensible, as Dennis's brother James once told me, "to white secretaries than to Negro teen-agers." This church—"the gift of the dead rich to the living poor," Bob always said—was where men trained in the intricacies of theological dialectic, men who wore cassocks and cottas and brocade chasubles from the religious closets of other centuries and other lands, led prayers in language like "propitiation," "made flesh" and "lamb of God." This building, where for more than a hundred years men and women had come, to kneel thankfully or to sit stonily with nothing about which they could feel grateful, to doze, to search for comforts that life had refused, to rest, to whisper, to be happy, to weep—was it a kind of home for Dennis and others? Was it a source of strength for Dennis's big brother, James, a "good" boy, lonely because he was unwilling to join the neighborhood gang, sitting stiffly in a dark suit and tie in the back pew? Or for Mrs. Hogan, arrogantly prepared to defend until death the legacy of refinement she felt her deceased Episcopalian relatives and friends had bequeathed to these very walls? Did it strengthen the heart of Sally, Mrs. Hogan's niece, whose secretarial job was a fearsome eight-hour journey into a world that scared her?

We asked ourselves what made Grace Church different from a settlement house? Surely we weren't brimming over with professional casework skills, but the relationships in the "cases" we had did not terminate; technically there were no good-byes. There was enduring emotional involvement. We believed that with all its crashing ineptitude, the church made the "we" who lived in the Victorian rectory and the "they," our tenement friends, all "we"; at my kitchen table and at God's altar we broke bread together.

Our talk grew less abstract. Imperfect, vulnerable to satire, a very fragile community did exist. In our very early Jersey City days, it described the coming together of people on the front walk of the rectory, the talking around the kitchen table, the working together at the craft evenings, the applauding at television Westerns, the uniting on Sunday mornings. This was different from the fiercely loyal little parish of individuals who had clung together for protection against the assaults of the city outside. This was different because the edges of exclusivity were crumbling. The Dennises, the men who came for coffee or clothes, the gypsies, the Mrs. O'Briens were as much a part of the church as the Mrs. Hogans and Mrs. Powells, whose sanctuary it had been for so long. Implicitly, the amount of money in the collection envelope, the primacy of Elizabethan prayers, the hymns of milk and honey were far secondary to what the Church could be: a place of welcome, of mutual support, of talk and laughter. Exclusiveness may breed a narrow unity that is a mockery of love, but a community that encompasses everyone enlarges us all.

This huge church, with its mahogany pews and frayed cushions, its black-and-white octagonal-tiled floor dulled and cracked by heat, cold, and the steps of generations, was becoming, however falteringly, a kind of home, perhaps not for the first time, but again. Might Paul and I, newly mindful of the inequalities of chance, opportunity, love, find in it a place of hope? The church was an arena where community was being acted out. For all of us it was an offering of all our brokenness together; it was forgiving and being forgiven; and it made us all, in our separate yearnings and despite all our differences, one.

After two days away we returned refreshed. We had set up no schedules, concocted no grandiose schemes, but there were a few concrete resolutions. Mrs. Hyde was asked that week to become the first Negro in the all-white choir. We thought she could most easily smooth over the bumps that might result. Some Negro adults and many Negro children came to church on Sunday but, thus far, pretty much on a visitors' basis. We felt Mrs. Hyde's "official" presence would make some difference; she agreed. Prejudice was an occasion for her wry, stiletto humor, and she thought of many ways to trick "the enemy." Somehow you knew she had control.

Another decision was to make the services more understandable and alive. We had discussed all sorts of possibilities —extemporaneous prayers, a paraphrasing of the more obscure language of others, simple instruction, less stuffy hymns, dialogue sermons with the congregation asking questions.

The first Sunday under this new regimen was a bright September morning, the kind when people murmur, "Summer is over, isn't it? I can feel something different in the air." We were apprehensive about Mrs. Hyde's debut in the choir. Clarence, red-faced but sober, stood by the rectory fence watching Dennis and Horatio throw pebbles at the adjoining wall. He had just finished coffee on the porch. James was talking to Naomi at the lych-gate. They were together a lot these days.

"Hi, Naomi, James. Hi, boys," I said as I left the rectory on my way to church. I reached the sidewalk in time to catch sight of Mrs. Powell's Sunday-morning arrival. She was slowly rounding the far corner, exploring the crumbling edge of the curb with her cane. The St. Mary's crowd had rapidly vanished from their nine o'clock Mass by foot and by car, and Mrs. Hogan, crossing the empty intersection, caught up with her political opponent. I could tell that there was a sharp exchange from Mrs. Powell's gestures, but I was too far away to hear. Others were arriving, hurrying now, a few with newly pressed white choir vestments over their arms. The church bell had stopped ringing.

"I guess it's time," I said to Mrs. Powell, who had now joined me. There was a wild snicker behind me from Dennis, and I turned to see one of his hurtling pebbles narrowly miss Lucille sitting on her stoop with the Sunday paper.

"Stop it, Dennis, and hurry," I said.

Mrs. Powell muttered something about "colored kids" as James, Naomi, Dennis, and Horatio met us in the vestibule, but she beamed when Dennis greeted her by name. I felt a nudge in my ribs with the knob of her cane. I turned, and she beckoned me closer. "It's a wonder Catherine Hogan dares show her face today with all them Catholic goings-on." I nodded blankly. "It's the Holy Name Parade today," she snorted—"priests, monsignors, and all our elected officials, heh heh. I know the money that changed hands getting them their fancy quarters downtown. I don't dust them City Hall offices for nothing. Them elections is rigged. And if Ed Hogan was still alive, he'd be marching with 'em. Holy Name, my necktie—Holy Hague is what I call it," she said, referring to the city's notorious political boss. She sailed past me down the center aisle, cane held aloft.

People were seated in small clumps all over the church. The organ burbled softly. Mrs. O'Brien was there, huddled in a seat toward the rear, alternately dozing and waking with a start, at which time she would smile at no one in particular. I sat down beside her. Dennis and Horatio couldn't settle on a location. They shifted seats noisily two or three times before the service began, dropping prayer books and scurrying to pick them up. Naomi and James were seated, as usual, in the back pew. Mrs. Powell was in front, and Clarence was directly under the pulpit. By the time the service started, he was sound asleep, slumped down so that—save for one hairy arm grasping the pew—only the back of his nodding head was visible.

"My Sally helped Mrs. Hyde in the rehearsal," Mrs. Hogan whispered across the aisle that separated her seat from mine. "It's the first Sunday for a colored. Father's right—the church has got to serve these people."

Nathan arrived as the choir finished a hymn and slunk in beside Mrs. Powell, who scrutinized him, then extricated a prayer book from the rack and handed it to him.

"Psalm 68," announced Bob from the chancel steps, "verses 1-10, 19-35."

"My God," commented Mrs. Powell loudly, "we'll never find that one." Aside from a muffled titter from Mrs. Hogan, Mrs. Powell's remark went largely unnoticed.

The psalm in question accomplished, Paul began a story for the children in the congregation. This morning it was the story of Jesus chasing the money changers out of the temple. Whatever more profound lesson the congregation learned, the story did serve to switch attention from the presence of a Negro singing in the choir. Paul asked Dennis and another ten-year-old to come up to the front of the aisle, sit down, and pretend to count money. From ten feet away he rushed at them, charging them with being preoccupied with unclean money in the House of God, and Dennis and colleague scooted back, properly chastened. After this lesson, Paul made some announcements of the week's activities, winding up with a plea for helpers to clean the vacant lot near where Mrs. Hyde lived so that it could be used as a play area. A minute's silence, and Clarence's red, hairy arm rose from the back of the front pew.

"You can count on me, Father," he called out. With that he rose, shook himself, and walked to the chancel steps. Hesitating only a minute, he turned, put his arm around Paul's waist, and stood with him facing the congregation. Paul assured Clarence, whose moment of satisfaction was marred only by a wheeze from Mrs. Powell and laughter from Dennis's direction, that his help was welcome and he would be notified of the clean-up date. Clarence returned to his pew.

Before the service was over, we were to participate in one of the modernisms resulting from our vacation deliberations. In some colossal effort at togetherness, which sounded plausible enough when we had discussed it, everyone was to say one prayer in unison and then firmly clasp the hand of the person on either side of him. I was sitting next to the aisle, with Mrs. O'Brien on my right. The big moment came. We all said the prayer together, except for Clarence, who had already returned to his slumbering position and was invisible, shielded by the back of the pew, and Mrs. O'Brien, who was nodding sleepily next to me. I reached out to grasp her hand as we had been instructed. She awoke with a tremendous start, pressed my fingers in return and shrieked, "Pleased to meetcha!" (There are always uneven spots in every innovation, we said later.)

After the service, Paul, Kim, and Bob went to the door at the back of the church and talked to people as they came out into the startling noon sunshine. Mrs. Powell made a few stops down the aisle on her way out, rapping lightly on a portion of one or another person's anatomy to signal her desire that he listen. She challenged Nathan first. "I understand from Father that you done fine with the baseball again this year. Now if you clean up your language like you clean them vacant lots for ball-playing . . . ," she said. He grunted with an embarrassed smile. "Be good to your mother. You won't have her forever." Nathan sidled out through a pew before she'd finished. Unaware, she continued her regal course, stopping to prod me as I stood chatting with Dennis.

"Take care of that baby, God love her. My own baby died when she was two." The snapping eyes filled with tears and the straight little figure sagged, but only for a moment.

"And you done a fine job," she said to Dennis, giving him a playful whack on his rear. "Never did like too much talk about money, and you acted Father Moore's story out fine. Can't say as I been spoiled by too much of it."

Nathan was beckoning to me from the door. "Tell Father Moore I'll help with the boys' club again Tuesday," he said. "I'll come over to the house later to talk to him about it."

"Okay, Nathan, I'll see you later." I wondered what he was thinking, if he felt useful and needed here. Could he get strength here to struggle against the other influences in the city, to curb his wild anger at the world? It was presumptuous, I felt, even to contemplate changing other peoples' lives.

Mrs. Hogan interrupted my reverie. "Sally and I are going to have an affair for the choir members at our house and make a sample of Father Moore's ordination salad for them."

"That sounds wonderful," I said.

I caught Mrs. Hyde's eye as she came out of church. She smiled as if to tell me that the momentous occasion of integrating the choir had gone without a ripple. It seemed so monstrous—and ridiculous—that it had to be an incident at all. She and Sally Hogan walked arm in arm to the street with us, and both winked knowingly as Mrs. Hogan recited the chicken salad recipe to me. She wound up as usual with a list of her butcher's credentials.

The congregation was standing on the sidewalk in knots of twos and threes. Mrs. O'Brien leaned against the fence talking to some girls in the choir. In the rectory yard Dennis and Horatio were throwing a fuzzless tennis ball against the wall, with Mrs. Powell keeping score. Mrs. Hogan was going around to the choir members, asking each to her house Thursday evening. James and Nathan sat talking with Bob on the rectory steps—a racial breakthrough, I foolishly thought. Kim and Paul were hearing from Mrs. Hyde about a battle they were helping her wage against a recalcitrant landlord.

When I first heard the sounds of the band, my mind was full of sentimental thoughts: this was the way it should be—things were moving, people were concerned about one another. When the parade came within half a block, I read the gilt script on the purple banner—"Holy Name Society." The bugles flashed in the midday sun; the top hats of the Mayor and his commissioners shone. The conversation in our group gave way to a buzz of comment about the parade. Mayor Hague's successor—his nephew—whispered to henchmen right and left. It was the Hague inheritance big as life. A few of the Hague group turned away, there was more whispered consultation, and the band behind them blared a Sousa march. When they were almost past, the Mayor and two commissioners turned to us, bowed briefly without breaking rank or step, and tipped their top hats. Following suit, the monsignors in the second row bowed and ceremoniously lifted hats our way. Conversations resumed, the band turned the corner, and the rest of the Holy Name Society—some two hundred men in Sunday suits, a few bulging with hip flasks—filed past, a visible reminder of where political and religious power in Jersey City lay. I wondered if our little community held in its hands any kind of power at all.

But the front row of gentlemen, after their ambulatory caucus, had acknowledged us when they tipped their hats, and there were other signs that the city knew the new regime at Grace Church was there to stay.

The Canaan Salvation Church, where Dennis's mother and grandmother were members, invited us to a Sunday afternoon worship service. "Ain't never been no white people in that church," said Dennis when we told him about the invitation.

"*Neee*vuh," added Horatio.

The invitation came from Dennis and James's uncle, who was the minister of the church. He worked in an upholstery factory and preached at the church on Sunday. He was dressed in a dark blue suit, brocade tie, and white shirt when he came to call on us one weekday evening. The children were already in bed and we were eating dinner.

"Wilkins, Wilkins is the name," he said when I answered the door.

"Of course, you're Dennis's uncle," I said.

"My shift at the factory commences at midnight, so I thought I'd come round and bother you. Don't let me stop you eating. I'll wait right here." Bob, Kim, and Paul pulled their chairs back from the kitchen table and came to the door to greet him.

"Fine, fine, fine." The wrinkles of brown skin around his smiling mouth were pressed in seams of anxious politeness as he shook hands all around. Paul pushed a fifth chair up to the table, its marbleized blue plastic already torn from the summer's wear.

"I been in the bed all day, so I'll just stay on these two feet," Mr. Wilkins laughed.

We reacted in chorus. "Oh, please sit down, Mr. Wilkins."

"I'll pour you a cup of coffee, Mr. Wilkins."

"We certainly are fond of your nephew, Mr. Wilkins." Our voices were abnormally loud, like tourists trying to make themselves understood in a strange language. Uncertain of how to reach Mr. Wilkins, afraid perhaps that we might not get through to him, we gave a polite shove to each syllable, as if that might help bridge the gap between black and white.

"You're doing a fine job, fine. The Board at my church hereby invites you to receive our tribute this coming Sunday." He never stopped smiling. He smoothed his thick gray hair with one hand and leaned back against the refrigerator door before continuing. "We don't have money for children's programs and such, but we sure appreciate your efforts to help our children. Sunday evening will be a testimonial of thanks."

Kim told him we would be there without fail. Mr. Wilkins shook hands all around, smiling and laughing. We urged him to stay, but he said he had to rest and eat before work.

"Fifteen years of those fumes for a man sixty years old is hard work." He laughed again. "We wear masks to protect us when we put that old stuffing in the chairs—you folks might not be familiar with an upholstery factory. Then I got the Lord's work Sunday—" a chuckle—"but you do the Lord's work for my people the other six days."

Kim, Paul, and I went. Bob stayed to take Evening Prayer at Grace Church. Sally Hogan came to baby-sit and answer the telephone in the rectory.

We walked with Horatio the six blocks to Canaan Salvation Church, down Newark Avenue, the central shopping street, and over to a little diagonal alley that was completely Negro. The frame buildings were nondescript, of no particular color. People sitting on stoops looked at us as we went by. Sometimes conversations stopped abruptly. On one flight of steps we saw a little boy playing by himself with a piece of string. There was no door on the house, and the hallway loomed cavernous behind him. He looked at us with big, faraway eyes and did not return our greeting.

The church was frame, too, and located a few doors down from where the boy sat dangling the string between his knees. Some of the steps to the door had been rebuilt recently, and the fuzzy new lumber gleamed pale apricot in the afternoon sun. Dennis was waiting for us.

"You early," he announced. We followed him into a low-ceilinged rectangular room. In front was a table covered with a white cloth. A metal vase with pearl-colored artificial flowers that resembled lilacs with no foliage stood in the center. Next to it was a golden-oak lectern, the ball and claw of its pedestal visible beneath a fold of purple material. On either side were brown tin standing lamps. The bulbs under the heavy metal shades gave the room a strangely white glare near the front, and left the rest in hot semidarkness except for the slits of afternoon light from the small windows. Mr. Wilkins arrived within minutes, and we told him how nice the church was. Dennis grabbed my hand and pulled me outside.

"James is here." James's self-consciousness at our presence was so apparent that it helped me contain mine. He had on the same pressed blue suit he had worn that morning to Grace Church. Dennis, holding my hand, twirled me around on the sidewalk and pointed at a group approaching. "There's my mother." Mrs. Smith spoke softly to me and welcomed me to her church.

"Mrs. Moore, proud to have you worship with us. Meet Miss Julie and Miss Helen, my friends. You all heard Dennis and me tell about Mrs. Moore." From the inside of the church behind me, where Paul and Kim were chatting with Mr. Wilkins, came the sound of a low song. The words were indistinct, the tone warm and throaty.

"That's Brother Wilkins' daughter singing," Mrs. Smith said.

Women started arriving with infants and small children. There were only a few teen-agers besides James. The two or three men present wore black or dark blue suits like James's. The majority of the congregation consisted of older women. I knew most of them by face or by name. Their welcome was warm and direct. They spoke of Grace Church and what it had meant to their children. I walked in with the women, releasing Dennis's hand with reluctance. Paul and Kim were already seated on two chairs in the front row. The singing became less formless as others joined in, although there were no songbooks. It was humid, and people fanned themselves with pocketbooks. I sat toward the back with those I knew from our craft program. Dennis was directly in front of me. From his seat near Paul and Kim, Mr. Wilkins started reading from the Bible. The singing continued. There had been no starting point, but the service had begun.

The Bible-reading seemed part of the song—warm and effusive. The spirituals, now more distinct, dealt with the joys that come after suffering, the peace that replaces turmoil, and they promised that Jesus will always find a way. People started swaying, and sometimes a single voice would rise above the others to affirm a phrase from the song. Each of my hands was clasped by the woman on either side, and with Dennis turning around every few seconds to check my performance, I moved my body with the swaying row. Mr. Wilkins, arms extended in front of him and hands clasped, eyes tightly closed, spoke of us as the new brothers at the beautiful stone church. "It looks like a palace to us," he said, "but it is indeed a house of love." Without changing position, he asked Kim and Paul to speak to these words. They stood and talked in turn, of the children we had grown to love, of the brotherhood of man.

I could barely listen. I wondered if I would be invited to

stand as well. Before I had time to think, I heard Reverend Wilkins, in a loud singsong, announce that the brothers and sisters would now hear from Sister Moore. I disengaged the hands clasping mine and rose unsteadily to my feet. Dennis was visibly thrilled and looked up at me with wide-eyed confidence. I could see Kim's and Paul's backs stiff at the front of the room. Mr. Wilkins stood, slightly swaying, with head bowed and hands pressed together. The singing became low humming again. I felt awkward but moved by the intensity of feeling around me, the unself-conscious expressions of the people in the congregation. My voice had that quality that mystery stories describe as "disembodied," but it came out. I told them what it meant to us to be there, and was answered with loud amens. I said that I believed there was a deep bond between us all in our belief in Jesus Christ. My voice faded off in a vapid sort of way and I sat down. I wondered if I really believed that He was the strength of my life. Could I compare my faith to the wholehearted passion in this room? I felt hot and a little ashamed, grateful and yet cross that I had been embarrassed. My introspection was cut short as people began to surround me, their hands outstretched. Before Mr. Wilkins, eyes tightly closed and head raised up, finished his extempore prayer, almost everyone had managed to touch my hands or arms in welcome. Paul and Kim were similarly surrounded in the front of the room.

When the service was over, we asked people to visit us and our church, thanked Mr. Wilkins for his tribute, and walked home, leaving the small congregation still chatting among themselves on the street.

I had seen shocking and sad things since we had arrived. There had been funny moments. But that day I was aware that I had been primarily an onlooker at the scene. Now, all of a sudden, I recognized myself as part of it. So much had happened in little more than a year.

The children were on the street playing ball with Sally when we turned the corner. The baby, nudged reluctantly awake by our voices, stirred fretfully in her carriage. Paul locked the heavy carved doors of the church. Harry was waiting for us in the kitchen. "My God, Mommy," he whined, "you been gone a long time."

XIII *"Nigger Bitch"*

By the beginning of our third year, almost everyone on our immediate block was resigned to our presence. Our own children played up and down the sidewalk. I was not the eternal sitter-outer on the stoop like Lucille and the others, but there was women-at-the-well prattle when we met. Our walk to the subway or to Howdy's was no longer silent. Most people had a greeting or would engage us in conversation.

Honor had her sixth birthday in mid-fall, and we asked the half-dozen small children on the block to come for ice cream and cake. Almost all of them came, although the mothers, despite our urging, wouldn't come any closer to our kitchen than to push their children across its threshold. "You have a lovely child, God love her," waved Lucille from the walk when her little boys came trooping in, handing Honor a new baby-doll with a plastic nursing bottle stuck in the pink brussels sprout of its mouth.

But the fist-clenching and the theological tirades of Mr. D'Agostino, the undertaker across the street, had not ceased. No amount of hat-tipping or attempts at small talk about the weather produced more than a sullen glare. Bob told us about the visit he paid him. Mr. D'Agostino rocked wordlessly in his chair while Bob stood out the silence leaning against the large murky plate-glass window, the dusty gold letters, "Funeral Parlor," above his head.

"What is it that bothers you, Mr. D'Agostino? We'd like to be your friends," Bob said after his "Good evening" received no response.

Shrugging his shoulders, Mr. D'Agostino stopped rocking and got to his feet, shaking his finger. "He ain't-a no saint," he declared angrily.

"Who's not a saint?" asked Bob quietly, disregarding the extravagant gestures.

"He ain't-a no saint. I walk by the church window, and there he is—in stain glass. He ain't-a no saint—a bishop's hat —poof! You got no bishops—you hate-a the Pope—you phonies!"

Bob explained carefully that we did have bishops, we didn't hate the Pope, that the window pictured recent bishops, and the one portrayed for posterity in the mitre was a venerable early twentieth-century gentleman called Onderdonk, who, Bob declared, had great respect for Rome.

"Crazy, that name," grumbled Mr. D'Agostino. "He real bishop?" Bob assured him that he was.

"Lousy black kids," he added, taking a new tack. Bob, still patient, told him the Church—his church and ours—should serve all people, that the children playing on the block had nowhere to go, that there were more serious problems than noise in the neighborhood.

"Crazy name your bishop—lousy black kids—but you nice man." He sat down again.

"Let me know when you have complaints, and we'll do what we can," continued Bob. All at once, the rocking chair was still; a mysterious smile played around Mr. D'Agostino's lined face. He pulled at a heavy gold ring with his right hand as though it were a magic talisman.

"Maybe someday we have a little wine together." Bob agreed and they shook hands. But Mr. D'Agostino wasn't entirely satisfied. With both hands he tugged the high black lapels of his jacket, as if to cover the heart that forgave too quickly. His voice was quiet. "To think I make-a date for wine with phony priest." He dug his heels in the sidewalk and set his chair in motion once more. "But you nice man." Bob hurried back to tell us of his triumph.

The ice was broken; the Bishop Onderdonk window gathered dust unchallenged by diatribes from across the street. Mr. D'Agostino had angry outbursts through the years, he shook his fist at kids rounding his corner, but much of his fire was gone. Most of the time he rocked, the huge rubber plant curling upwards in the show window behind him. The proposed wine party was never held.

On another front we were also making a little progress. We were seeing more of the Negro parents whose children were in the organized evening groups, at church on Sunday, or just around. Some adults, usually brought by their children, visited Grace Church on Sundays, and others, such as Mrs. Hyde, joined the confirmation classes. Although they never seemed really relaxed there, Mrs. Smith and Mrs. Trotter came faithfully to the frequent guild meetings called by Mrs. Hogan and devoted to decisions about how many olives to put in chicken salad, and whether paper napkins should have scalloped edges. Nonetheless, for them, the church their children went to became a place of real attachment, a place that could provide help in the emergencies of fire, eviction, hunger. For others it represented simply the place of the handout. We knew this and worried about it sporadically, but we grew to accept it. We couldn't do anything else.

The coexistence between black and white in the parish was still uneasy. Nathan and the other members of the white baseball team (which had slowly petered out this third summer) associated with Dennis, James, Naomi and the other Negro children only during activities within the church, parish hall or rectory. Beyond those walls, they ignored each other. The turning point was adolescence. "I hate the niggers," the typical little white boy next door said, and kept on playing ball with Dennis. It worked when they were small. With the boys who had reached puberty, tension ruled. The black-white relationship stopped, for all but a few, just outside the school and church doors. On the street you were black or you were white, and you chose your friends accordingly. The boys—all of them—thought we in Grace Church rectory also had to choose. Except for organized encounters of black and white adults and adolescents, Mrs. Powell's prediction, made two years before, of two churches was correct. It was painful to acknowledge, but it was a fact.

Despite our visit to Canaan Salvation Church, despite the constant association with Naomi, James, Dennis, and the others, despite the problems their parents occasionally brought to Bob, Kim, and Paul—despite all of this, there was a difference among ourselves, too, between our relationship with white people and our relationship with Negroes.

On our part, we were patient with the Negroes, often overcompensating with excuses for any fault, and we had a nagging fear that no matter what we did, we'd feel guilty. About the Negro poor we said to ourselves, however privately, "It's partly our fault"; about the white poor it was, "I wonder why they didn't make it?"

The Negroes did not show any obvious desire to be left alone, or open hostility to us, or even ambivalence—it was more a reserve, or an inability to catch the white glance. Mrs. Smith told us of her difficulties with the landlord, of how money was hard to come by, of her dependence on James, her elder son ("He helps me more than his father do"); but she did not wallow in the intimate, emotional revelations that Mae and others poured out in our kitchen. The Mrs. Smiths of Jersey City spent much time in our house, but they did not use it as a forum for their feelings. She and others like her might make an appointment with a priest to talk privately about a problem; usually, however, we had to seek the problems out. When visiting in a Negro area, Paul, Bob, or Kim would stumble upon a situation where they could help. Had they not, the church would not have become involved, because Southern-born Negro adults were reticent about exposing their real grievances to us. Perhaps they did not trust us enough; perhaps they had no hope that anything could change for them, and only the slimmest of hopes and dreams for their children. The matching furniture, the grand clothes, the new houses that they saw on television belonged to white people with fancy educations. The Mrs. Smiths might as well have aspired to the moon as to all of that, the one was about as attainable as the other. Perhaps theirs is the last Negro generation to take the imbalance lying down.

Nor did the Negro adults seem comfortable with the free-wheeling discipline that prevailed at our house on Second Street. It was almost as if they wanted to protect us from their children's behavior. It was never discussed except in the most formal manner, but I'm sure that those who did keep in touch with where their younger children played would have opted for something stricter than our inconsistent enforcement of rules about noise and curfew.

Grace Church was like the mother whose yard is the center of activity for her children's friends—"At least what happens goes on under my nose." Each night of the week a different group met—little boys, teen-agers, younger girls. We were no longer trying to supervise everything ourselves. There were more and more volunteers, giving a night or more a week, helping with recreation, Sunday School, or whatever best suited their talents. In those days, the whole operation was unusual enough to produce publicity, because the Episcopal Church, except in a few isolated and magnificent instances, had done little in downtown areas after the "Episcopalians" had left. Articles in church magazines and in newspapers, word-of-mouth, the speeches we were asked to make—all aroused interest and attracted people to Grace Church.

One of our new volunteers was Derek, a young actor whom Bob knew from earlier days. After an initial success on Broadway, he had bounced from disappointment to disappointment, always thinking the part for which he was not quite hired would have repeated his headline hit. He had sustained himself for five years largely on alcohol and the growing memory of his one role. When we first got to know him, fame's last layer had peeled off; nothing was left—no confidence, little money, no hope. So Derek had come, at Bob's urging, to see if there was any interest in dramatics at Grace Church.

Word spread that a real live actor was anxious to start a production, and soon Derek, as director, producer, and chief supporter, was putting on one-act plays with Nathan, Naomi, James, Mae Corey, and others in the cast. Derek worried over the rehearsals as though a new Stratford were in the making. The cast fussed over him with the same care. They were concerned when he had been drinking. They told him their troubles, they listened when he recounted again his long-ago success, and—what was new for him at that moment in his life—they prized his attentive love.

The rehearsals took place in our living room or the parish hall kitchen, depending on where the actors could be assured of quiet. Months later, after feverish ticket-selling, the finished production would be put on. The plays were always melodramas, with James and Nathan—getting along well enough in this structured situation—alternating as black-caped villain or corn-fed hero. Mae was invariably the twenty-year-old ingenue, and Naomi, the innocent younger sister. The rest of the cast varied.

At the performances, Frank and the Corey children would sit in a row, watching Mae perform as though she were at long last the dimpled heroine with a life of easy choices between right and wrong stretching clear and beautiful before her. Mrs. Powell sat in the same front-row seat, somehow sacrosanct for her since her bell-ringing part in Harry's first nerve-crushing performance as Santa Claus, and she would manufacture suspense with hoarse whispers and motions of her cane. Inevitably there was a curtain crisis, with Harry and Dennis pulling at either end, the audience roaring advice. And afterwards, audience, director, cast—especially the last two—would tell each other how wonderful it all had been.

Giles Tompkins, an English antique dealer, was another volunteer. He was introduced to us by the assistant rector of a midtown Park Avenue parish. He was anxious to teach carpentry and arrived alone for an interview at Grace Church, dressed in a houndstooth tweed jacket in mid-July. His face was long and handsome until he smiled, when suddenly his chin shot forward like the base of a right triangle, making you fear that he might never be able to pull it back again. When the jaw finally quivered into place after his jovial "How do you do," I was able to concentrate on amenities.

"What is your job over here?" I asked, catching sight, out of the corner of my eye, of Harry ambling in the door. He stood in the front hall, directly behind Giles, and cocked his head, first over one English tweed shoulder, then over another, making silly faces at me. Giles, unaware, was regaling me with his autobiography.

"Oh, it's antiques all the way, but it's taken some time. First public school—straw boaters—rugger—the whole shooting match. Then I was interested in public service." (Harry's eyes were tightly closed, his mouth set in an inane grin, a silencing forefinger pressed against his lips.) "I'm passing the summer in Manhattan with a firm that shows highboys and the like—Queen Anne's my specialty—but I'm sight-seeing really. My hope is that some Yankee patina will rub off on *me.*" Giles' giggle was shrill, and he slung the jaw out again.

Harry joined in the laughter, jumping up and down. "We fooled him, didn't we, Mommy? He didn't know I was here."

Giles turned in his tracks.

"Jolly joke, Grandpa—you part of the staff here?"

"They can't do without me, that's one sure thing," Harry said proudly.

"We certainly can't," I answered, mildly apprehensive that Harry, with one of his double takes, would suddenly react to the "Grandpa" title and go into a foot-stamping rage. Age was a tender point with him.

Paul emerged from the living room to greet Giles, and the front hall conversation evaporated, Harry taking his broom for a go-round on the front walk, Paul and Giles adjourning to the living room to discuss the carpentry class. I was sure Paul was wondering, as I was, if the class wouldn't prove, for teacher and students, to be the unbridgeable culture gap.

Paul reported to us later that he had his doubts about Giles, but suggested we give him a try. They had settled on a class in metal- and woodwork for a group of boys in their later teens like James and Nathan. The older boys would not show up at all if something didn't appeal to them. On the other hand, if they were interested, they would fling themselves enthusiastically into an activity. We thought they would be easier for Giles to handle than the younger boys, who were often discipline problems. We had very few criteria for volunteers other than friendliness, a little talent, and that great imponderable, reliability. Giles seemed rather an oblique fit, but never mind—he had already made simple designs for objects boys could make, he had raised money in the New York parish for the necessary tools, and he throbbed with enthusiasm.

Wednesday at seven was to be the first meeting of the

class. Word was passed via Nathan and James that Giles would be available if anyone was interested.

"Rotten hot and humid, isn't it?" said Giles when he arrived on the dot. "Brought wrenches, saws, and the like over with me on that underground you have from Manhattan to Jersey. A corker, isn't it? Could you fetch my lads?" We looked at one another. The idea of "fetching" the teen-age boys for a formal presentation to Giles seemed precious. Instead, Paul led him, with his clanking satchel of equipment, over to the parish hall where some boys were shooting baskets. He came back amazed that they had responded with alacrity to working under such an unlikely leader.

Giles stuck his head in the rectory after the class. "Great show! Daresay I could work up a team to repair London Bridge if there were time. Real talent there tonight. They want me back tomorrow—then we'll get a real toehold on the projects. We touched on rudiments of technique tonight." We were astounded. A lecture on technique, and they had asked him for another session right away?

We made fun of him, I'm afraid, as he left, bounding down the front walk—the kind of Englishman Evelyn Waugh would dismiss with half a caustic line.

Giles returned the next evening. The boys were waiting for him, and attendance had doubled. Nathan, Billy, and Eddie, who had been present at the technique session, did not appear. We chalked it up to boredom. The boys who took part in Giles' class that night were James and his friends, and they were all Negro.

Nathan and his two inseparables, had been hanging around since the end of school, uninterested in baseball this year, they said, and unable to find jobs. We took them at their word, not sufficiently aware that where Grace Church had once been neutral territory, it was now becoming a black and white proving ground. For a month, after activities had closed each evening, we had watched these boys and others standing on the nearby corner in racial knots before dispersing for the night. They were members of loosely formed white and black gangs that roughly corresponded to the housing patterns. We knew there was tension, but we didn't know how much. On the second carpentry night we found out. Giles had joined us for supper in the rectory before his class. Dennis looked serious when he ran in.

"Gonna be trouble with Nathan's crowd. Even James is going to fight."

"What a bully errand! A little tyke bringing the news from Ghent to Aix, eh? Good show!" said Giles, looking up from his custard.

We took Dennis half seriously—he boasted often about what he heard on the street—and we were surprised at James, who prided himself on not joining any gang.

While the carpentry class was meeting, Paul and I stayed in the kitchen and pieced together a more complete picture from James himself, calling him over from Giles's class after it had begun.

James was handsome in a stolid sort of way, overburdened with helping his mother and now-unemployed father take care of Dennis and the six other brothers and sisters. He never spoke much, and this night was no exception. Finally, however, we learned enough to corroborate Dennis's account. James's girl, Naomi, had been insulted by Nathan outside Howdy's candy store earlier in the week. Nathan had been joined within minutes by ten or twelve white boys, so instead of engaging Nathan in an immediate fistfight, James, accompanied only by his friend William, had agreed to a gang rumble at a vacant lot later in the week. It was scheduled for tomorrow, James finally admitted. He couldn't be dissuaded. All his reservations about gang life were suddenly in the background. Nathan had called Naomi a "nigger bitch." James would entertain no discussion about a change in plans and excused himself to rejoin Giles.

Paul had just phoned the police from the rectory to warn them there might be trouble when Giles blew in.

"Just taking a breather—no H_2O problem, is there? I say, Jersey must have stolen some hot weather from Florida," he said, snapping on the faucet with a flourish. There were heavy beads of sweat on his high, pale-pink brow, and his brown hair was lank from his exertions. He drank a glass of water with a smacking of lips.

"The fellows seem more interested in metal than wood this evening. Busy as bees with hacksaws, making axles for their autos. They brought in pipes—jolly ingenious."

Paul hurried over, to find the basement empty. The class had left by the other door, "axles" in hand.

"Sticky wicket, ingress and egress at opposite ends of the hall" was Giles's comment when he arrived on the scene. Paul commented sharply that it was too late for architectural regrets and that doors or the lack of them couldn't stop a riot. Giles smiled nervously. "A real 'Dover Beach' is it? 'Where ignorant armies clash by night.' " His poetic analogy fell on deaf ears.

Giles went home to New York, and we went to bed, not knowing how seriously to take the new situation.

In the morning Dennis came by for his usual breakfast visit. "Mamma don't know it, but James and a big crowd are goin' to kill all those white kids in the vacant lot at four o'clock. James come in real late and gets into bed with me. He be tired today."

We questioned him. "Did James tell you all that?"

"Me and Horatio was in that hole under the stoop, and we listened. James sounded real mad. William was along, and he said, 'There's not gonna be no Nathan left!' "

"How do you know the time and the place?" Paul asked.

Dennis had an answer for everything. " 'Cause William

say the police always look for trouble after dark, so they plan it for when it be still light. They said four o'clock on Maxwell Alley, I heard 'em."

Kim and Paul passed on the information about the fight to the police, and the presence of two of them at the rendezvous dispersed the few boys who had arrived as advance men. The police phoned to suggest we were crying wolf and said everything was under control.

The next step was for Paul and Kim to go to a bar where they knew Billy, Nathan, and Eddie hung out. Bob remained at the rectory to deal with information as it leaked in from Dennis and others. The bar, Paul said, was frequented by truck drivers and was in an all-white section halfway between the Holland Tunnel entrance and the rectory. It was dark, heavy with smoke and the odor of tired men. Art, the bar's manager, was aware the boys were underage, but he never sold them beer out front; they helped him clean up and, in emergencies, bounced rough customers. Nathan felt his presence there greatly enhanced his stature.

In the early evening at Art's bar, Nathan agreed to participate in an eight p.m. peace talk in Bob's room at the rectory, if Paul and Kim would escort him through what he termed "the nigger lines." There was not long to wait. At the appointed hour, Nathan, flanked by the two priests, walked the few blocks. The scene didn't have the color of a Hollywood set, but all the other elements were there: Kim and Paul, their black shirt sleeves rolled up, their white clerical collars a bit wilted in the summer heat, both looking young, handsome, and earnest; Nathan, his stride longer than usual, with tight blue jeans, cowboy boots, his toes turned slightly out, thumbs locked under his heavy belt buckle—all suggested a poor man's *High Noon* with benefit of clergy. And leaning out on window sills in the background, a couple of old Italian women, their inevitable black shawls pushed back from shoulders encased in more black, pointed at the priests in this surprising role. Little children playing in the gutter stood up startled, pail or ball in hand, to watch the trio go by.

As they approached the church corner, James's friend, William, and three other Negro boys came out of the parish hall and stood across the sidewalk, leaving only a small space free next to the curb. Nathan stopped for a fraction of a second but did not look up. Paul and Kim spoke to each of the boys by name and the boys returned the greeting, looking ninety per cent deadly serious and ten per cent ashamed. Nathan was silent and followed Paul and Kim single file through "the nigger lines" into the rectory and upstairs. Within seconds, it seemed, James had been notified that the peace talk was almost underway, and he ran up the two flights to Bob's bedroom.

I had put our children to bed earlier and, while peace was being discussed on the third floor, was in the living room with the teen-age girls' club, the door closed. It seemed wiser to allow the girls to meet as usual, considering the explosive possibilities of their being on the street and the fact that Naomi was one of the members. As a rule, Naomi was cool; tonight she was silly and irritable. All the girls, about twelve in all, were in their teens; tonight they pinched one another and whispered like six-year-olds. Even Louise had withdrawn behind an impenetrable curtain, her whispers private and exclusive. We reviewed plans for a summer dance that the club was sponsoring. I found myself in the dilemma of not wanting them to sense my alarm, and yet wanting them to be aware that there was real danger in their racing out to the sidewalk before the conclave upstairs had finished its deliberations. It was beginning to grow darker outside, and the girls peered out from behind the drawn shades at the street. They made no comment. For the first time in months, I was an outsider. It was as if our long period of friendship had been burned away by Nathan's two words, "nigger bitch."

The whispering didn't stop when Paul opened the door of the living room to tell us that James had received a reluctant apology from Nathan. He told me to wait ten minutes and then it would be safe to send the girls home. Then he left, closing the door.

Little did he know. Dennis, Paul Revere-like, had been on the prowl again and had seen what he described as "hundreds of white boys" walking up Erie Street two blocks from the church, with sticks, stones, and "even guns." There were rumors at Howdy's candy store, he said, that Negro boys were on their way from another part of town to join James's local battalion.

The police arrived soon after to confirm Dennis's news, describing the number in scores, not hundreds, but substantiating his report of weapons. They said that, short of using violent methods themselves to disperse what was now an almost mob-sized crowd, they were helpless. Paul told them of the handshake agreement that had been reached on the third floor and, along with Bob and Kim, succeeded in persuading them to hold off for the time being.

In the heat of the moment, none of these developments had been passed along to me. With all the female din, I was unaware, as were the girls, that the police had been to the rectory, or that the street in front of the church was swarming with armed and angry boys. I was running out of patience with the hot and inconclusive club meeting and told the girls to clean up the pop bottles and straws. Paul's ten minutes were almost up.

Meanwhile, the three priests went out on the street. The whites were on one side with their homemade weapons, and the Negroes, "axles" in hand, were stretched across the other. A police car drove up, and Paul, Kim, and Bob persuaded the police to let them handle the situation. The leaders of both sides stood close together exchanging phrases, the opposing groups sullen and tense around them. James and Nathan repeated their upstairs decision that a fight could be avoided and that no one's turf had really been invaded. Tension diminished.

At that point, believing things quiet, I let the girls leave. They ran out squealing and giggling into the group of boys. Bodies bumped against one another. Passions rose with female shrieks and loud male voices. I stood at the lych-gate, rooted to the ground in surprise and disbelief. After what seemed like hours, but was in fact only minutes, lines were drawn again, and the girls were persuaded to go home. Tension subsided without violence. A movie finale found the leaders shaking hands once more, with the police, Paul, Kim, and Bob looking on. We drove various groups of boys in our station wagon to points near where they lived, and at last the street was quiet.

Nathan, Billy, and Eddie drifted away that night and were never back with the same feeling of belonging. They came by when they were in trouble; they came to church once in a while. Occasionally they dropped by the rectory to chat about the early days. It was a hard fact to swallow, but as far as gangs of teen-age boys in Jersey City were concerned, we had finally found we couldn't be all things to all people. The psychological victory belonged to James that night; the teen-age white crowd had been decisively defeated.

XIV *"You'd Think You Was Lonely"*

The gypsies, who had come again in mid-February, 1952, were right that time, too. I was pregnant again, and Mamma, pressing her ear, gold hoop and all, against my protruding stomach, had said, "A leetle girl again—makes you happy in old age." I had no retort for "old age," but Rosie did arrive that leap year.

With our family of four children, we filled up the three bedrooms on the second floor. Kim and Bob occupied the two front rooms on the third, and the little bedroom adjoining theirs in the rear was for visitors—who spent a night or two, or stayed, like the man who came to dinner, becoming part of the landscape for a year or more.

The year after Rosie was born, Kim accepted a job with a church on New York City's lower East Side. There were tears, going-away parties; the four years had passed quickly. We decided to wait before looking for someone to take his place.

An immediate result of his departure was an extra bedroom for overnight guests.

When Mrs. Roberts and John Henry came, it was summer. A policeman phoned at about four in the morning to tell us a mother and son were sitting at the bus station. The bus authorities had notified the precinct that they had been there almost twelve hours. "They haven't even left to take a pee," he told Paul. "We're used to some of them that just come up from the South thinking they'll land a job for two dollars an hour doing nothing. The woman looks like she's not good for much but laundry work, and the kid's only fourteen. She's Roberts—Annabelle, or some long jigaboo name. The boy's John Henry. They're the only people at the station, except two fags in and out of the men's room."

After complaining that they hadn't chosen to call earlier in the evening (we never gave the police the benefit of the doubt), we agreed to go down and at least offer them shelter for the fraction of the night that was left. We dressed hurriedly. The beginnings of morning light showed in the sky as we drove to the terminal. It was almost empty when we arrived, save for one sleepy ticket clerk; the "fags" had vanished. Mrs. Roberts and her boy sat in the middle of a wooden bench directly under the one harsh overhead light. Either end of the long bench lay in heavy shadow. John Henry was looking down at his foot and kicking at the long loop of clothesline wrapped around the brown cardboard suitcase. When Paul introduced himself and said we had beds for them, Mrs. Roberts moved stiffly from her seat as if she had been touched by an invisible wand. John Henry seemed reluctant to leave. Mrs. Roberts lifted the suitcase, but the boy's foot continued kicking, now at a pink gum wrapper on the concrete floor. Mrs. Roberts stood silently, holding the brown case under her arm, although its size made this awkward. Paul and I urged the boy to come with us and have something to eat; he did not react. Finally, a nudge from his mother brought him to his feet. When we came to the door of the bus station, she lifted her arm from the case and with both hands gave it to John Henry. We walked through the exit, Mrs. Roberts directly behind us. The heavy door of the terminal closed between the boy and his mother. Moments later it heaved open, and John Henry appeared and looked around bewildered, pausing for a second to adjust the case in the cradle of his bare arms as though it were as delicate as the dawn that greeted him. We drove through the quiet streets to the rectory. Neither of our passengers spoke except to answer "Alabama" in low unison to our question about the home they had left.

Mrs. Roberts was very disturbed. Once John Henry had eaten and the suitcase was safe in the third-floor bedroom, she began wringing her hands and speaking in low, desperate spurts. She told us that she had ridden the bus in search of something and now she couldn't find it. No, she assured us, loosening the hair that had been coiled in a wispy bun at the back of her neck, she had had no job promised her, she knew no one in the North. She didn't know why she had come, and she repeated over and over that she had $7.30 in her string purse. We persuaded John Henry to go to bed and took turns sitting up with her. Her fears grew uncontrollable, and her anxious fingers combed frantically through the hair now flowing about her shoulders. John Henry woke after a few hours, seemed oblivious to his mother, and shrugged his shoulders when we questioned him about her.

By noon, Mrs. Roberts's speech was unintelligible, and we took her to the psychiatric ward at the medical center. Bob, Kim, and Paul took turns at her bedside. The intern told them he could do no more than sedate her and hope she'd be well enough to return home. "I see cases like this every week. They work up some promised-land complex about the North and end up psycho, boozed up, or broke—or all three."

Leroy, one of the older boys, who had driven to the hospital with Paul, insisted on helping to soothe her during her long terror-ridden day. The nurses were only too glad to have extra help.

Leroy was something of a problem himself. He was obsessed with the idea of being a bastard. When we first knew him, he had discovered that the woman who had brought him up was not his mother; the birth certificate she had said she was keeping safe for him did not exist. He didn't know who he was. Louise used to try to comfort him. "Leee-roy," she crooned, "I changed my name—I mean my big thithter changed my name over the thummer. Leroy, it don't make no differenth anyway—you thee, I uthed to think my thithter wuth my mother." But, unsmiling, Leroy told her that he didn't see it that way, that it did matter. When he had held Mrs. Roberts's hand, he told Paul, he had felt that he was part of the world for the first time, that he had helped heal someone.

Mrs. Roberts responded to rest, food, and medication. John Henry stayed at the rectory the two days his mother was in the hospital. Embarrassed that he was unable to scratch his name in the dirt when challenged, he spent the time alone, eating every crumb that was put before him and bouncing a ball off the wall next door. His jeans were more faded, the trouser legs much wider than the Jersey City boys'. ("Them farm boys are funny," said Dennis.)

When the hospital released his mother, Paul brought her back to the rectory. Her hair was in a bun again, the eyes were softer. She thanked us politely for our kindness, picked up her brown rectangular case, nodded to her docile son to follow, and insisted on returning independently to the bus station. We watched them go from the kitchen window.

"Beats me," said Harry, as they rounded the corner. "Now there's some folks that really come out of the blue—isn't that so, Mommy? And now they're going right back into it."

There were more permanent visitors, too. Sadie Perkins came to live with us because her three-room railroad flat was destroyed by fire and all her possessions lost. She was willing to move into a white household because her friend, Dennis's mother, knew us well. If the fire had happened our first year, Sadie would not have come to us. It was one thing for us to house the Lee boys, victims of the coal bin fire, but quite another to offer a room to a Negro adult. For that, there had to be long-term trust.

Sadie was short, with black eyes and gray permanented hair. She left the rectory at five in the morning for her job in the Tootsie Roll factory. She laughed a lot, especially with our baby, Rosie, but the smile left her eyes when she joked that she had two strikes against her because she was half Jew and half Negro. We picked up her story slowly. She was rejected in early years because she was a Jew in a Gentile neighborhood, mocked when she was in high school because her teen-age friends found out what she had not known until then—that her dark olive skin came from a Negro father who had deserted her mother when she was a baby.

She stayed with us over a year, months after she had saved the money to rent some more rooms. We still lacked the confidence to risk hurting her feelings by suggesting she move, although Dennis's mother scolded us for being "soft on Sadie." She finally left of her own accord, growing bitter at the world and critical of the all-Negro neighborhood where she lived. "I've got the lightest skin on the block," she told us. Years later a Christmas letter came, proclaiming proudly that she had a room in a white boardinghouse on an all-white block in Atlantic City. She really didn't care, she wrote, that she didn't see anyone from one end of the day to the other. She had just enough money to live on, and she did some baby-sitting for her landlady.

Sometimes we had boys in the house for months and years at a time—never planned, never part of what, in our occasional moments of evaluation, we thought we *ought* to do. We had watched it happen around us: a family would be evicted, another already overcrowded family would take them in without hesitation. We could not do less.

Other people than the whites left in the neighborhood and the Negroes in the downtown area surrounding us began to be attracted to the church—Charles Beckwith, for instance. Charles was ten or fifteen years older than Paul and the only Negro in the parish during our eight years there who had professional training. He was a lawyer, practicing in a more prosperous part of the city. He belonged to the NAACP, and represented the first leadership that was not from the area, the first evidence that more privileged Negroes were watching.

Light-skinned, moustached, in a dark gray suit, and with hat in hand, he came to inquire about the confirmation class which he said he had read about in one of our church notices in the paper. His speech was precise and formal. When I urged him to come in, he did so but seemed ill at ease, holding the rim of his hat in both hands so his knuckles made a little archway on the dark felt. We chatted briefly, and I directed him up to the third floor where Paul was conducting a class for a bunch of teen-age boys lolling around in blue jeans. Charles put down his hat and listened.

In those few moments, he became a strong supporter of the church. He generously gave legal counsel in housing and other situations, and was always chivalrous with Mrs. Powell, but it took great effort for him to understand Dennis and the other boys and our laissez-faire discipline—he wore his formality like a suit of armor.

Neither militant nor satisfied, he was modest in hope and in appearance. He was a lawyer who had worked hard to get where he was. Mrs. Hogan started right off describing him as a "high type" and never put him in the "second-best china" category. It was a sacrifice for him to step down the social ladder and leave his middle-class Negro Baptist congregation for a largely lower-class Episcopal church. Yet Grace Church was doing something, and he had made up his mind to find out what. He fought alongside the clergy for better recreation and integrated housing, and against police brutality.

Some—usually the people who had thought of the church as a Jane Austen establishment that reserved its welcome only for an exclusive few—were drawn to Second Street when they found the rectory door was, in effect, always open. Others were attracted by the informality of the church services. Although some of our innovations in the services, like the "Pleased to meetcha" episode with Mrs. O'Brien, were somewhat awkward, many others added meaning as well as gaiety to the liturgy. Sometimes Paul preached from the pulpit with Bob asking questions from the aisle, often on topics of social concern in the city. Members of the congregation were free to comment or criticize, or bait the preacher. Some were attracted to the church by the endless variety of people—the Louises and Naomis, the families of eight and ten children, the gypsies, the small circle of elderly white ladies, couples like the Coreys, and individuals like Harry and Mrs. O'Brien. We were visited by those of high and low estate who had heard of the church: an English physicist, who corresponded with one of Dennis's sisters for years after his visit; an English monk with thonged sandals ("I seed his big toe *and* little toe," said Louise); an Indian bishop who wore handsome pink robes and mesmerized the children when, at dinner in the rectory, a kernel from a cob of corn he was munching became embedded in his heavy black beard.

One winter, a photographer from *Life Magazine* descended on us for three days and took pictures of everything—church services, rectory meals, parish hall basketball, the arsenal of knives and blackjacks we had taken from the boys after minor fracases, feebleminded Horace repairing Rosie's high chair with a wooden tray he'd found in the dump, Mrs. Hogan having a tea party (*best,* not second-best china). For months afterward, the photographer used to come regularly and visit us and his new Jersey City friends.

Like Charles Beckwith, Megan Maura Marconi was also an "outsider"; she wrote us a letter giving her reasons for traveling to Grace Church from another part of Jersey City: "You have not allowed form to stifle content. . . . Even the station wagon shows the same spirit. It could have been a snob in the suburbs without sacrificing form to content, but think of the fun it would have missed. . . ."

The letter, with its personification of the station wagon, was a little affected, but we were intrigued. Who was Megan Maura Marconi? Certainly she was like no Jersey City-ite we'd met so far. The letter was typed on white linen paper with an embossed monogram, "MMM," at the top. The signature was a nest of wavy ellipses—the "successful businessman" kind of signature.

We didn't have to wait long to meet the author of this missive. Early one evening, only days after the letter's arrival, Megan Maura Marconi came up the walk. I heard her laugh as she turned to watch the children playing in the yard. She came in the door without ringing and poked a blond head with a high, wide brow into the kitchen.

"Just as I thought—" and then that laugh again—"you're all ministers, you're all drinking beer, and Mrs. Moore looks like a tired debutante. Form not stifling content again." We were all stunned. She was full-bosomed, round and white of arm, wearing the palest of blue V-neck cotton dresses. She shook hands all around and introduced us to a black-haired, black-eyed girl of about four who was holding onto her hand.

"This is my daughter, Ariel."

Ariel's big eyes registered the same kind of abandon as her mother's laugh. "Do your children have dolls?" she asked, peering into an empty playpen strewn with stuffed animals. I took her upstairs, where my children were playing before bed, and left her, hands on fat little hips, surveying the children's toys.

Maura was perched on a high stool when I came back. She turned to me. "I was explaining why I wrote the letter—I need to be involved. I live here with my mother-in-law—Joe's mother, she never let him grow up. He's away in the Merchant Marine—he hates the church because she wants him to go—you know the type. Ariel and I are coming here, that's definite." Confidences tumbled out: an early marriage to a Park Avenue doctor and their country club life in Connecticut; her divorce; a series of jobs as telephone operator, nightclub hatcheck girl; finally Joe and home in Jersey City in an Italian section ten blocks from us. She sighed deeply.

"Joe's a child. He loves to cook for Mamma and play with Ariel. He likes to play with me, too," she laughed. "But I want more out of life. When I worked at the Copacabana, I used to talk about existentialism with the customers. My God, Joe can't get past the funny papers. I suppose I was in love with my father—who isn't, after all? He didn't get any pleasure from my mother; she was always there to love me and my sister, to give us security. My father was unstable—from him we had nothing but insecurity. They're both invaluable, you know—security and insecurity—if you get them both early enough to develop your character."

Her life in Jersey City was full of pasta, her Italian mother-in-law, and Joe, when his ship came in. Maura loved her street, its noise and the Italian vegetable carts. She was aware of her Negro neighbors in the blocks bordering the tiny Italian section and made a point of being friendly—not much in itself, but unusual in that neighborhood. She cared about individual dignity, and she thought Grace Church was a good place to express that concern. Her toughness, although genuine, was no protection for her loneliness. She had the classic Marilyn Monroe quality—like the actress whose initials she shared, a part of so many worlds that she really belonged to none. She looked at her life as though it were a tapestry into which she was always trying to introduce another color, and she threw the whole rug at anyone who would listen.

Mrs. Powell resented the influx of adults, feeling that it made her a less prominent figure around the rectory. Sometimes, indignant that animated conversation was going on in the kitchen among people she didn't know, she would stalk out without sitting down, saving her verbal displeasure for the following Sunday.

"My God in heaven," she would declare, "you'd think you was lonely, needing people around you till ten o'clock at night. I never seen nothing in the Bible about having people of different colors running around a church twenty-four hours a day."

And Harry, too, grew rattled by the numbers. "It just don't make sense, Mommy. We could have a whale of a good time, just you, Poppy, me, and the family—and here you want to have a crowd doing things all the time."

XV "*Look For Me in a Red Cravat*"

In the early fifties, with the funds from a large undesignated financial gift to the diocese, Bishop Washburn bought a tenement house on Second Street for Grace Church. Its floor plan was similar to that of all the other houses on the block—four floors, with three rooms on each side of the stairwell. Offices and rooms for Sunday School classes, craft sessions, and meetings were to be on the first floor, and more of the same on the second. The third floor consisted of a double apartment, which eventually housed a young priest and his wife who came to take Kim's place. On the fourth floor was another double apartment, one room of which was converted into a tiny chapel. This was soon occupied by three nuns belonging to an Episcopal order. The order provided the small stipend necessary for them to maintain themselves, and they worked full-time for Grace Church. Their duties included visiting families, running the Sunday School, and organizing the camp program, which had rapidly grown from a dozen children in free camps to about a hundred going to a variety of camps. The presence of the sisters made quite a difference in the attitude of the people on our block. Although there were still complaints about too much noise, too much activity, and too many children, the real antagonism, the fear, and the stony silence of the first years were only memories.

The sisters' rule did not permit them to speak between the evening meal and breakfast; they attended the regular public services of Holy Communion and Evening Prayer, and also had, each day, required periods of silent meditation and prayer. They were at least middle-aged, removed by the traditional nature of religious life from the world—from civil rights, politics, foreign affairs. Nuns were not yet on picket lines; there were no freedom marches. They loved the ancient forms of prayer; they didn't fuss, at least out loud, about the anachronisms of church services, or question, as we did, the relevance of the institutional church. Their ignorance of worldly matters occasionally had some startling results. Once Sister Mildred Eleanor was taking care of the pets belonging to an elderly parishioner who was in the hospital. "I'm just a regular cathouse keeper these days," she noted. On another occasion, the same sister, quite deaf, was chatting with Paul and me on the sidewalk. He was summoned by eight-year-old Sammy, Dennis's brother, in a flurry of importance. "Father, Father, one of the new kids is peeing off the roof!"

Without giving Paul a chance to comment, Sister patted Sammy's head. "Boys *will* be boys. I bet you used to do things like that all the time, Father."

But the quaint stories were incidental. The point was that these women loved with a discipline, a single purpose. The kind of love of which they were capable cut through taste and personal preference and was revealed warmly and directly. They prayed for people unfailingly. They tried to bear the burdens of grief and suffering and injustice in acts of kindness. Their rule of chastity, poverty, and obedience did not imprison them. On the contrary, it freed them for love.

In the same building in which the nuns lived, a psychiatric counselor came one day a week to see a small number of patients from Grace Church, and volunteers tutored children after school in remedial reading, mathematics, and other subjects. (Louise said, "I never underthtood an ithotholeth triangle before.")

Another project was sex education. In one of his early books, Thomas Merton says there is no difference between illicit sex under a silken coverlet in mid-Manhattan grandeur and casual intercourse on the rooftops of Harlem. Morally, no; in fact, no; but the attitudes involved are worlds apart.

I had grown up in a society where the unmarried mother is kept under wraps with an aunt who lives in another state, or, in more affluent circumstances, she is whisked off to Arizona or Europe. (Arizona seemed to be the answer to so many things. I remember as a child thinking of it as a place that could boast of nothing but abundant cactus, dry air, and the mysterious arrivals of anonymous females.) Above all, the condition and its termination were never discussed, alluded to, or admitted. In Jersey City we had to grow accustomed to the acceptance of pregnancy no matter what the circumstances. It was a more honest system than concealment-at-any cost, but the multi-generational households it led to, where the various fathers were often unknown, served as a further wedge between the culture I had grown up in and theirs.

In any event, we decided, when we were first confronted by teen-age unmarried mothers and realized that yet another generation of children was growing up around us, that we should provide a course of sex instruction for the boys' and girls' clubs. It was an insufficiently planned, superficial little episode.

We had thought a young physician could communicate more easily with our Jersey City boys than the established, middle-aged doctors we knew, but the intern who came to us through a New York friend was even more naïve than we were. The night he arrived to speak to the boys he was exhausted and pale, with a dark, two-day beard. He insisted that Paul stay "until the discussion starts moving." He tried to communicate, all right, but the vernacular he spoke wasn't the language of Second Street.

He began abruptly, Paul said. "The male is differentiated from the female by the fact that he has a penis"—pause—"that is to say, peter." This was the first of many startling observations he shared with the boys in the course of his lecture, which was of the biological geography variety, punctuated by brief intakes of breath and the phrase, "that is to say," followed by whatever slang term seemed indicated. The boys lolled around and laughed among themselves as he spoke, only occasionally asking a question. By common agreement, it was one of our less successful projects, and the intern did not return.

The girls' visitor was a psychiatrist from a New Jersey hospital. She had a hyphenated name, something like Winfield-Winton. When she arrived, I led her down the staircase to the rectory basement, where a dozen girls were dancing to records. The music blared, drowning out their voices and mine.

"Girls," I shouted above the noise, "here's Dr. Winfield-Winton." They went on dancing. (I had told them earlier in the week that she was coming over to talk to them and answer questions about sex; most of them had reacted with soundless assent.) Naomi lifted the arm of the record player. The room was quiet.

"I'm Dr. Winfield-Winton. Dr. Winfield-Winton has come to talk to you girls. Dr. Winfield-Winton is from Eastern State Mental Hospital," said the doctor, sitting square-toed on the old swivel chair in the dark basement. Naomi examined her long tapering fingers, affecting inattention. Gradually the rest of the girls found a windowsill or chair to sit on. The doctor and I had prearranged that I would not stay for the talk. As I left, she was still filling them in on her credentials.

She was white, confident, efficient, full of ready information, and wore her yellow hair straight, with bangs. She would spare no detail, I could tell. She would be devoid of the kind of sensitivity in which we wallowed about the gap between white and black cultures. I wondered if the girls would give her the same attention they gave to their grandmothers, who told them about men, filled them with the fear of God, and gladly took care of their babies.

When she discussed the girls with me afterwards, Dr. Winfield-Winton's manner was warmer, and she had something to say about each one. She was struck by the quantities of misinformation the girls had about sex, thinking menstruation a punishment, kissing the source of babies, and intercourse an irrelevant pleasure. As she left, the doctor told me that Naomi—"that lovely thin-boned girl"—would be the first of the group to become pregnant; most of them would become pregnant before marriage, she added.

Afterwards, Paul and I talked about what she had said. I mentioned her prediction about Naomi, chalking it up to book learning rather than experience. But it was not very long before Louise came, full of importance, to report that Naomi's baby was due before Easter. I remembered Dennis's song:

> James and Naomi up in a tree,
> K-I-S-S-I-N-G.

I remembered James walking her home night after night after church activities, and at the lych-gate, their soft voices and shy hands moving in the dusk.

After Louise's report, Naomi came and sat at my kitchen table. "I hear Louise told, but I only did it twice." She stared straight ahead. We couldn't talk. It hit me harder than when the other girls brought home babies. I had had dreams for Naomi—but they were my dreams, not hers.

Paul tried to persuade the mothers at the least to postpone the marriage, but James and Naomi, teen-age children, became man and wife. Weeks afterwards, Naomi told me how scared she had been on her wedding night, which they had spent in a bed in her mother's apartment. She said she had pressed her body to the wall and pretended to be asleep when James had come up from the street below. I had to assume that being together in a doorway was different.

Dr. Winfield-Winton returned a couple of times, but attendance dwindled. With the press of other things, we did not attempt any more sex talks. Deep down, I think we knew a lecture series would have had little effect on James and Naomi making love.

But other new programs were added, old ones were stepped up. As the programs grew larger, they made more demands on the slim resources of the church. The budget was severely strained.

Grace Church had an endowment left over from its well-heeled youth yielding three thousand dollars a year, but technically the church was an aided parish, which meant that at some point—long before we arrived—it had not been able to support itself or keep up its financial obligations to the diocese. Responsibility for maintenance and most financial matters therefore reverted to the Bishop, with the understanding that the parish would work to reach self-supporting status again. The parish worked, all right, but the money simply wasn't there in Jersey City.

"Look for me in a red cravat and a white carnation. I will be on the noon train from the Jersey Shore," wrote one of our more picturesque contributors. "I like what you're doing. I've read about it in the newspapers. Cordially, J. A. Pettis, M.D." Paul wrote back that we would meet the train the doctor had designated. All we needed was Victoria Station to make it pure Alfred Hitchcock.

We watched a small rotund man clamber down the train steps, look long and hard each way down the station platform. We had brought along Louise, Dennis, and two of our children, and they stood hand in hand, gazing in wonderment. Dr. Pettis was ruddy-faced and carried a cane. The carnation was white, and the tie was red, as he had promised. Paul introduced himself. Dr. Pettis handed Paul an envelope and quoted verbatim the end of his own letter: "I like what you're doing. I've read about it in the newspapers."

Paul thanked him profusely, but was waved firmly aside. Dr. Pettis turned on his heel, tucked his cane under his arm, and climbed back on the train, apparently planning to sit until it clanked its way to South Jersey once more. Paul opened the small unadorned envelope. Inside were five new hundred-dollar bills. The children touched each one admiringly. "God," said Louise, "do you think he keeps it all under his pillow?"

For five summers the same ritual was enacted. Dr. Pettis wore the same identification—white flower and red necktie—advising us ahead of time with a terse postcard, "Arriving Newark with contribution, J. A. Pettis, M.D." Each time he pressed the five bills into the palm of the person commissioned to meet him. The sixth year the appeal we mailed to him as usual, describing the church's summer plans and activities, was returned stamped "addressee unknown." That's all we ever knew.

Frequently there were contributions after speeches one or another of us had made, and often the donor, like Dr. Pettis, would keep on remembering the work each year. Other parishes in the area were exceptionally generous with checks and with presents for Harry's Santa Claus sack at Christmastime. Larger donations from family and friends were made usually in response to the special annual letter.

Money-raising affairs were put on by the new and the old members of Grace Church. Mrs. Hogan ran card parties and bazaars, which collected a pittance; James, Naomi, and their friends sponsored city-wide dances, which provided a small but regular income. In the summer, the volunteers put on a massive field day with athletic events, cake sales, baby contests, and the rest.

So we limped along, accused over and over, because the church was interracial, of being "Communist-inspired." It was wondrous to me that our group of a couple of hundred downtown Jersey City residents—only a few with cars and telephones, less than half with high school diplomas, and scarcely more than a handful with college educations—could be regarded as conspiring to overthrow, in the halcyon Eisenhower period, the Government of the United States—even with those firebrands in the rectory!

XVI The Children's World

Our children thrived. Except for summer vacation in the Adirondack Mountains and a weekend now and then at their grandparents' farm, 268 Second Street in Jersey City was home. The concrete yard that had replaced the green lawn in front of the rectory was their playground. They had friends among the children in the houses on our block and in the tenements in the neighborhood. As the years went on, it was the children's relationships up and down our block that continued to soften the hostility toward our noisy compound. An English family moved in next door and started coming to church, causing our older neighbors to look at Grace Church with new eyes. The fact that a white couple on the block belonged to *that* church reassured people. The little English girl, named Maria because the *Ave Maria* had been sung at her parents' wedding in London, became Rosie's best friend. Maternal communication on the block increased to such a degree after the British arrival that four mothers, including Lucille and me, invested in a huge community sandbox for the rectory yard. Once more we were roundly defeated by the cats, but they weren't able to contaminate this first real Second Street alliance. Briefly, at least, it was our block against the cats, and the unity against the common enemy left a layer of intimacy and goodwill that outlasted the feline victors.

Our children did not live amidst green grass; they did not have trees to climb. They lived in a world of city options: playing hopscotch, bouncing balls, hydrant "swimming," skipping rope, and joining in the never-ending doggerel of sidewalk games. Ours was the only front yard on the street, so their activities were always in full view. The teen-age gang troubles were never in any way connected with violence or hostility toward younger children. Pip lived in Jersey City until he was ten, and his closest friend was Dennis's brother, Sammy. They still correspond, and they see each other now and then. Our four elder children remember things unusual for children of parents whose own childhoods had been full of arranged afternoons of play, governesses, and creamed chicken at birthday parties. They remember brushing by foul-breathed drunks in our little front porch when they wanted a glass of water in the kitchen. They remember the cats, the clattering trash cans, people standing around when they were eating breakfast, lemon ice at the candy store, and going to bed earlier than anyone else. They remember my hiding until Christmas the many presents from uncles, aunts, and grandparents that flooded our December mail, but I'm not sure how aware they were that no one else got packages.

They have memories of crowded Sunday dinners, with guests from the parish who lived alone or were in trouble, or with some of the volunteers who called Grace Church home—and amongst them all, Harry, either grinning contentedly or stomping around saying nobody loved him. They remember the weekends at their grandparents' farm thirty miles away, where things were orderly and clean. And I guess they recall that a good deal of the time, Mommy was having a baby.

Until 1957, our last year in Jersey City, when our own family had grown large enough to occupy every corner of the house, there was always a teen-age boy living with us. (Our youthful boarders were all male; it never seemed helpful when dealing with the problems of the Negro girl to remove her from home. Early promiscuity or pregnancies before marriage might sadden a mother, but they were not regarded, as they might be by the white middle class, as shameful. In those days, when the mantle of Southern acceptance of things-as-they-are still hung heavy, the Negro girl expected to do much as her mother had—care for babies, go to work, help care for grandchildren as they came.) Our children treated the series of boys in the house with the same combination of awe, admiration, irritation, and lack of interest that they might have accorded an older brother.

Once it was a Negro boy who had been in the hospital for a period of months with suspected tuberculosis. His father had died of it. The doctors wouldn't permit him to go to his mother's basement flat with its damp floors but allowed him, with regular checkups, to come to us. He stayed two years, until his mother, who had been on the housing project waiting list since the beginning of his hospitalization, was finally assigned rooms. Everything broke right. He was over sixteen, so he was able to go to school and work part-time, contributing a little toward his board at the rectory and giving the rest to his mother. He didn't feel like a charity case. It made a difference that he came to us from the hospital and not from the streets. He was able to like us and love his mother. He could cope with Harry's tantrums and the Moore children's chaos. He was not a "goody-good"—city gang life tempted him and, as the hospital days grew more distant and the street closer, it was harder for him to resist. But he married young and happily, and finished college while working. He is now an executive of a settlement house, the father of four, and he is active in politics. He was fortunate. He had a stable mother who cared, the ability to respond, and, for a time, the enforced removal from the streets when he was ill.

But why some make it and some don't remains a mystery to us.

Another long-term visitor was a white boy whose alcoholic mother made him tend the house, mind the other children, and beg for change to fill her pocketbook. At fifteen, he would ring a doorbell, pretend to faint, and, if someone took pity on him, he would ask for pennies as he revived. With his mother's permission, Ronald came to live with us, and his younger brother became her next begging performer. Paul worked closely with the Welfare Department in Ronald's case, but they were loath, as we were, to remove any of the children permanently from the mother. After psychiatric help and a minimum of responsibility in our household, Ronald was able to return home with the strength to refuse some of his mother's demands, despite her rage. Shortly after he went back, he was old enough to go out on his own. But for years now he has had no address. First there were postcards to the brothers and sisters, all living with a modicum of security; now they have no idea where to find him. He is as anonymous as the brown-eyed beggar he used to be on Jersey City doorsteps.

Sometimes our young boarders came for only brief stays—after arrest and consequent imprisonment, or eviction, or tragedy. It was always a shot in the dark—we never knew if we could help or exactly what was accomplished. Even now we wonder. Sometimes, the freedom of the house, the fact of our personal possessions, and the unspoken barriers at which we could only guess combined to accentuate a boy's problems. If he had any history of stealing, he stole more. Often he couldn't handle the reaction of his peers to his living with us in the rectory. Or it made him silent and tight-stomached to be expected at table at a certain hour to sit through a meal, informal as ours were, instead of serving himself from a pot on the stove when he felt like it. Conversely, the very factors that seemed to destroy some made others stronger. Some of the boys, faced with a more definite daily schedule than they had ever known and with meeting new people each day, took it all in stride. There was no way to predict or to measure success or failure.

Because of the communal life and the constant traffic of people in and out the front door, we were rigid about what little privacy we had as a couple and a family. Breakfast and lunch, though never private, were relatively quiet. The hour before bedtime, provided someone was available to answer the telephone and doorbell, was a time to retreat upstairs for prayers and stories. Midway through our eight years in Jersey City, we discontinued our custom of feeding the children early and all ate together. There were always guests, interruptions, and spilling; the meals were exhausting and fun.

Each successive child seemed to take more easily to this life of ours. For Honor, almost four when we arrived, full of energy and make-believe, it was the least natural. We never would know where her intensity, her devouring of books, her playacting, her adult air all came from. She would plunge into the box of dress-up clothes we kept upstairs and, costumed in ragged finery, promenade with her doll and carriage up and down the sidewalk, dodging trash cans and Lucille's little boys, wondering, we always felt when watching her, why the world around her didn't join her parade. She would fling herself with sweat and tears into every project. In second grade, her teacher asked the children for samples of different materials. Honor believed in following such requests to the utmost. She cut small pieces from sheets, socks, her father's shirt, a sneaker, a comforter (taking a feather or two for good measure), bedspreads, curtains, her sister's clothes—little was spared except her own possessions. The teacher gave her an A+ and sent home a note that she was "immensely resourceful." I agreed wholeheartedly and went into a rage, which recurred each time I found a textile with another small square removed. Such discoveries went on for years.

Pip did things very differently. While Honor wept over *Black Beauty,* he played ball with Dennis and Sammy on the street; while she rubbed crayons to a stub on endless sheets of paper, he announced, with Olympian majesty, that he would never draw, and he never did. When Pip was six years old, he was given a cowboy suit for Christmas, which aroused Harry's jealous wrath (he stalked off to rent some Marine blues in order to equal the child's grandeur) and Pip shed a few uncomprehending tears. But that was it; from then on, he met Harry's volatile ego with silent tolerance. When, instead of the desired baby brother, a third sister was born and Honor organized a flap of doll parades, Pip said with gospel fervor, "God lied."

Dee was born soon after our arrival in Jersey City, into the typically relaxed environment of the third child. She never dissembled. She took things as they came, without the shifting of mental gears that we, as adults, had to do. Everyone was the same in her eyes, and she acted accordingly. At her helter-skelter birthday parties, she would introduce the grimiest child to the most soigné relative present as though she were presenting royalty to royalty.

When Rosie arrived, Paul took me to the Margaret Hague Hospital—built with "dollars stolen from the likes of me," Mrs. Powell always said. The elevator girl gulped at his clerical collar in the maternity ward in this Roman Catholic citadel. On the way to the delivery room, I was wheeled through a large room filled with long tubs, where moaning Negro mothers in labor were scrubbed and told to wait their turn to give birth. I was a private patient, but Rosie was a public baby, and she laughed her way through her crowded rectory babyhood. When she was not yet one, she visited jail with me. It was a Sunday. She was sitting on my lap in church, and Louise came running and hissed in my ear during the singing of a hymn that William, James's friend, had been arrested. She said all he had done was watch a knife fight late Saturday night. We were wary of the police; they had kept boys illegally before. With Rosie perched on my hip, I left church. James drove us to the jail in our station wagon. Chucking the baby under the chin, the policeman took us to see William, who confirmed what Louise had said: that he was standing on the street and was picked up along with the two knife-wielding men. The cop seemed doubtful, when pressed, that he had the right to hold him in this fashion as a material witness and, with a prod from lawyer Charles Beckwith, released William later in the day. I wondered whether the police would have let him go without prodding. I doubted it.

After Rosie came George, Marian, and Danny, who were three years, sixteen months, and six weeks old respectively when we finally left Grace Church. Their Jersey City life was limited to the playpen, a birthday party or two, church, and a few sallies to the candy store. They were born in Morristown—I couldn't face again those tubs of anguished women waiting to give birth.

We sent the four oldest children to the local public school six blocks from our house. Dennis and his little brother, Sammy, accompanied them. The public schools were uncrowded in those days because of the heavy parochial school population. We had Honor tested at one of the leading New York City private schools after she had finished the second grade; she had accomplished as much as her Manhattan counterparts in most areas of study and was ahead in a few. When Honor finished fourth grade, we found ourselves concerned not about what she was learning but about the lack of competition, and we sent her and Pip to an Episcopal parochial school in lower Manhattan, one stop on the subway from Jersey City. They were shepherded over in the morning by parishioners who worked in that area, and they traveled back by themselves.

Together, Paul and I worked hard at "after-supper time" with the children, apprehensive that they might grow to hate the many people they shared their parents with. It was not hard to tell them that Christ was in the face of the poor—it seemed so real to us. We taught them that the church was concerned with the whole of life, and it was no abstract precept when we reminded them that the breath they smelled on the front porch of their house belonged to people whom they could not ignore.

Occasionally I overdid it, like the time I bought a pamphlet about religious life in the home. When it arrived, I was appalled to find that it advocated ordering your child to choose his favorite Christmas toy and "sacrifice it to the poor." I threw out the pamphlet.

XVII *"Hey, Mommy, Did You Give 'Em Hell?"*

"Your husband was so profound—and he must have so much pressing on his mind—and you certainly told some funny stories." The lady in the white straw hat and print silk dress squeezed my arm as she spoke. I glanced over her shoulder at Paul, surrounded by women, teen-age girls, and a few men in business suits. We were in a pseudobaronial parish hall in Montclair, New Jersey, the kind Mrs. Powell had described so long before as having "carpets in the halls"; Paul and I had been invited here to talk about our work in Jersey City before a large gathering of suburban church congregations.

"It must be a real sacrifice bringing up your children where they can't have friends," another listener said.

"Oh, they have lots of friends," I answered, giving her one of my weak smiles. I had described the city and its people and our philosophy of the open rectory, peppering my talk with little anecdotes about Harry and Mrs. O'Brien. At the end, I had spoken of our children and how the ones who were old enough were part of all the neighborhood activities. Yet the only thing this woman had grasped from my talk was something that hadn't been said at all—that my children had no one to play with. My oversensitivity was surfacing again; I knew it. Yet I was also aware that those who had understood what I had said, who had looked briefly over the rim of the world I had described, would forget it all before they drove back into their pebbled driveways.

I was still frustrated that I had been unable to communicate my feelings when Paul's Cousin Helen found me at the tea table, choosing between henna-colored brownies and cherry-centered cookies on scalloped paper napkins. I was surprised that she had come.

"Well here you are!" she exclaimed. "I drove miles from Far Hills to hear you—I was due in New York anyway, so this wasn't too much out of my way. Marlon Brando's movie about the dirty streets—all those bums and the picturesque rooftops covered with pigeons—isn't that where Paul's church is?" Cousin Helen talked on, not waiting for an answer. "It's an old movie—you don't have to tell a buff like me—but anyhow, we finally saw it in Florida, and I told Bill, 'If we look hard enough, we'll spot Cousin Paul in one of those saloon scenes, turned-around collar and all.' He preaches to all *kinds* of people, doesn't he?"

"It doesn't matter to him what *kind* of people they are," I said. "And being preached to doesn't make sense when you're down and out." (I hadn't known I was so irritated until I heard my own voice.) "He tries to help people get jobs, to deal with cut-throat landlords and welfare problems." Cousin Helen was smiling at someone over my shoulder as I spoke, but the phrases tumbled out. "*On the Waterfront* is about Hoboken, but the church is in Jersey City—very close-by. You can take the subway from New York."

Cousin Helen looked around the room. "Aren't I lucky to have you to myself for a few minutes? Now—do you live in the same place as the church, or does Paul commute? I couldn't tell from either of your speeches."

"We live next door," I answered. "The rectory is part of it all. It's a way to get to know people, to be in the neighborhood—you can't live miles away and have the same identification. We wouldn't do it any other way." I was angry that she hadn't listened. Cousin Helen patted my arm, but her blue-eyed gaze was vacant.

Paul joined us. "There you are," she said, "handsome as ever. 'Going my way,' beautiful?" She patted Paul's arm. "A Bing Crosby movie—dates me, doesn't it? I haven't seen you since you were married. How long has it been?"

"More than twelve years," said Paul. "How's Bill?"

"As husbands go, he's great. Bit of a spare tire round the middle, but what do you expect for half a century? I wish he were here to learn about that wonderful work you're doing and those cute children. I had no idea until I talked to your Jenny here that you lived right there, although I had heard there were pickaninnies running in and out of your house. Aren't you lucky to have married a wonderful Lady Bountiful?"

"Oh, Cousin Helen," I interrupted, "that noblesse oblige stuff is just what we want to avoid." I could hear my voice rise in annoyance above the buzz of conversation in the room.

"This is my chance, Paul—tell me how the church operates. Will you be promoted someday if you're really successful—I mean to a place that will be better for the children?"

"That's really up to us. I have other offers now and then, but we want to be there—the kids really love it. Rosie always says she likes hydrant-splashing better than swimming in a pool. . . ."

"Here we are gabbing," Helen broke in as Paul spoke, "and lots of other people want to talk to you. I was crazy about both your speeches. . . . You know what Bill says when we talk about you, 'Lucky as sin Paul Moore's rich enough to spend all that time in the slums.' " She got up quickly and pushed her way across the room, carrying a glass of punch on a level with her blue-gray upswept hair.

"That's my favorite exit line," said Paul wryly. We both laughed.

There were other groups, usually women's, that invited me to speak. Often, surrounded by polished antiques in suburban living rooms, I felt that I talked too long and in too much detail about the people on Second Street. I told of Naomi's mother's devotion to her retarded son and how, right or wrong, implicit in her strong feelings against institutionalizing him was her patient love. While I was talking, I could imagine Dennis beckoning me from the window to come up and meet his mother that first time, and his eagerness as he introduced me and the children—"Mamma, this is the Moores." I told funny stories about Harry, of his appearance as Santa the day the reindeer died. How could I go on to say, so that my audience would take me seriously, that the rectory was Harry's only home in the world after the circus had moved on without him? I spoke of men who came to the door and asked for coffee and overcoats. I felt like a shaky bridge between the men I saw in my mind's eye trembling from the effects of alcohol, lifting cups of coffee to faces slack with despair, and the attentive ladies to whom I described them. Sometimes a number of the audience, honestly sympathetic, would tell me she was a contributor to Planned Parenthood and inquire if I had any statistics on unmarried mothers in our area. I used to answer that I wasn't good at figures, that it was hard to talk about statistics when they involved teen-age girls who had grown up around our house. I couldn't forget Naomi, who had told me, "I only did it twice," or Mary, the retarded girl who had sat at our kitchen table the first summer and said, "Don't you think it's right, Father, that I'm giving it up? Horace says I'll get in trouble, he says I'll have a baby if I keep on doing it."

There were things I never could explain so that they would understand. Could I explain to them how we tried to enter the lives of destitute people—yet maintained middle-class attitudes about so much of our personal lives? Could I tell them that, yes, we knew our identification with the people in the slums had a loophole, since we always had the freedom to leave? It sounded so defensive to say so. It stuck in my throat to say I felt guilty that I was telling funny stories at the expense of people who were suffering, that I was saying anything at all about the people we loved—but the guilt was there.

I was never sure what I wanted of my audiences. They collected clothes, they sent money; some of them came over and looked around. But I wanted them to know that the gift of cast-off clothing is not enough, that tutoring one day a week is too brief a relationship. I wanted them to know that their values were not the only values; the mutual concern of city people—on the city streets where I lived—for one another, against the common hazards of eviction, hunger, and bloodshed, had taught me the meaning of the Christian gospel. I wanted them to commit themselves to causes that weren't then in vogue, to identify with lives that weren't really very pretty. I told them that being "churchy" was very different from being Christian, but the words seemed to hang in the air and flutter away unconsumed. I should have asked for their hearts and guts.

They always thanked me after I had finished and said how interesting the talk had been. One of the ladies would drive me to the train and I would try to sort out my reactions to those well-meaning people—inchoate, angry and confused then as now—as I rumbled home on the Lackawanna line, taking the bus from the Hoboken station to Jersey City. Sometimes when I stepped off the bus at our corner, Harry would be standing across the street next to his rooming house. "Hey, Mommy," he'd shriek, "did you give 'em hell at the whatcha-call-it meeting?"

XVIII *"Thought I Was Dreaming of the Old Days"*

We learned in our first year on Second Street that it is not enough to become familiar with poverty's face, for after that comes frustration as you find how little its features can be changed. And so our middle Jersey City years brought disappointments. We learned the bitter lesson that not all problems can be solved, that dull aches persist, and broken lives are briefly mended only to break again.

Mae Corey attempted suicide several times after the wrist-cutting of the first Christmas. We had to learn that she was never successful, that although we couldn't be callous, it would happen again. Dolores, her eldest child, had grown cynical in her teens. "She's trying bottles of pills now—the razor hurt too much. The only thing she ain't done is stick her head in the oven." Mae leaned heavily on the church, as if everything she did there was magically sanctifying, even to the taking of her life. She sang in the choir and smiled, diva-like, at Frank and the children sitting in the front pew. She acted in all Derek's plays, thirsting, as the day of performance approached, for him to say, "Bad rehearsal means good show," so that she could answer, with stars in her eyes, "We won't let you down."

Save for Dolores, the Corey children used some of our newly acquired camp scholarships and, during the school year, came to all the evening groups. Dolores had dropped out when she reached adolescence. Mae felt compelled to make excuses for her, and she told me one morning, "My Dolores grew up with the coloreds, so it really isn't prejudice, but that girls' club at church is *all* colored now, you know, and that's hard when you're the only one. She's nervous one of those big Negro boys will get fresh with her. Frank says, 'Dolores, you flatter yourself, girl,' but my Dolores says, 'Mamma, you always told us it's all right for us to play with them, but you don't want no coffee-colored grandbabies!' " Mae laughed. "I guess she's right and I'm a sinner—here I am complaining about coffee-colored kids and I'm a mixture myself, but somehow the Oriental background in the Islands is different. My daddy made me real proud. 'In Hawaii we practice what we preach about the equality of man,' he used to say. But here they don't seem to have no pride—the coloreds, I mean. Maybe that's the trouble—no pride."

Frank landed a steady job on a barge, but he drank more, and there were periodic separations. After each crisis, they came hand in hand to the rectory. Each time, Frank was red-eyed from the last drinking bout but tremblingly proud of Mae, as though a freshly shining world lay at her feet.

"We made up again." Mae would smile, sitting at our kitchen table jabbing out cigarettes in a little pile of lipsticked butts and holding Frank's arm as he lit her another. So life went on.

To be sure, there are Maes and Franks, no less pathetic, in comfortable brick houses in the suburbs. But the Coreys' moments of desperation, which occurred with such exasperating regularity and were unaccompanied by pretty clothes, verandahs, carefully groomed children, or even physical comfort, seemed more cruel and final. The blows were never cushioned.

Mrs. Powell rapidly became feeble. Watching her grow old, poor and alone, had a dull-edged sadness of its own. She retired from her cleaning job at City Hall and lived on a small pension. On her last day at work, the Mayor's office presented her with a shield-shaped plaque enscribed, "Winifred Oates Powell—Eleven Years' Faithful Service, 1943-1954." She brought it to the rectory to show it off. The more we admired it, the more critical she grew: "This here award don't mean nothing. Eleven years—the nerve of them down there! Seems like fifty when they're spent on your knees scrubbin'!" She spat on the end of her little finger and rubbed it over the coppery metal where her name was printed. "Initials spell WOP. When Willie was alive, he used to say, 'Winifred here is the first Protestant Eyetalian,' and then he'd laugh like mad." The wrinkles in her face grew deeper; she was seldom on the street except for church on Sundays and an occasional afternoon at the lych-gate. Almost overnight she began to need her cane for support. She no longer used it to thumb her nose at the seedy landscape of her world, to threaten Dennis if he acted up, or for fiery emphasis in her political dialogues with Mrs. Hogan. The gingery speeches were still delivered, but the words spilled out unevenly.

When we went to see her, the radio was playing too loud, and often with the cacophony of two stations tuned in the same time, as if each was battling for her old and careless ear. Sometimes she wasn't dressed and sat in her arm chair wrapped in a quilted robe that puffed out in little spots where the stitching had unraveled. The hair, which for so long had been secured with too many brass-colored hairpins or mashed tight under the lavender hat, lay loose on her back like a little girl's. When she opened the door for one of us, she always scolded her visitor for catching her unprepared, and then settled him or her down and asked for news.

"Don't mind the dark hole I live in, but I gotta watch the electric bill," she would say. Reminiscing, talking about the people she knew and slamming some of them—"And what kind of stories is Hogan telling these days?"—made her seem spry again. Before the visit was over, she would gather her hair in a hasty bun and pour a premixed Manhattan into two long-stemmed glasses. "My Willie Powell couldn't swaller one of these without a cherry, but I think they're too damn sweet as it is," she would say. After one sip she would nod sleepily, waking minutes later with a start—"Thought I was dreaming of the old days"—and she would be quiet, touching her body under the wrapper with a faltering hand. It was always the same. Sometimes the afternoon sun came in through her shuttered windows, and she would push the goblet across the table until it caught a streak of light. "My God, don't it shine!" she would say with pride. And the smell of old age was all around.

We found her body after the landlord called to say that he couldn't get into her apartment. The coroner said she had been dead at least two days.

Our middle years were marked also with disappointments that came from our own naïveté and inexperience. When Horace's sister Mary told us our first summer she was going to "give it up," I think we believed her. But eventually feebleminded Mary came by to show off her baby, whose father, still another sailor, had gone without her learning his name. "It was one of them Polish names," she said. "I could pronounce it good one time, but then the next time I don't remember—you know how it is, Father."

But Horace teased her. "The times you don't remember is the times he was promisin' the moon."

Mary looked down embarrassed and surprised us with her wit. "*Some* moon," she answered.

Horace said she never took her eyes off the child, and it seemed to be true. Together they had bought a shiny carriage on time. "It's copied after an English coach," Horace said. Mary sat for hours on the lych-gate bench, her hand on the high chrome handle of the carriage, rocking it back and forth. Pale blue plastic clips, with a cupid embossed on each prong, held the coverlet. All you could see was the baby's head, bonneted no matter what the weather, her little mouth working sleepily at the pacifier. Now that she had the baby, Mary told us she wasn't going to bother with men any longer. Horace would help her raise the little girl.

Horace was dutiful. Each day he came to walk Mary and the baby home. He never could resist bending down to grin at the child as he tilted the carriage, easing its silver-spoked wheels over the sagging curbs.

Paul's work in housing had grown more sophisticated since the small rent strike failed that first year. Housing clinics had been set up in five Negro neighborhoods. Each one was manned by one or more local residents responsible for dispensing accurate information about the rights of tenants both in general and in particular instances. Mrs. Trotter was in charge of one clinic at the apartment she shared with her daughter Naomi, James, and the baby. She kept the baby in the daytime while Naomi worked at the hospital as a dietician's aide, and at night she cooked at a restaurant. Mrs. Trotter said she always regretted she didn't stick it out against the landlord in the early days, "but I knew nothin' about it. You was new at the church, and I never seen no minister fighting with a landlord before. I just got scared." Charles Beckwith gave a great deal of his time to the legal side of the cases at all the centers, and through combined efforts of a lot of people many families were saved from paying illegally high rent; but sometimes the lawsuit against the landlord failed and eviction resulted. Like everything else in the city, it was one step forward and often one back.

Later still, Paul was involved in trying to break discrimination in low-cost public housing. With Charles Beckwith, some Jewish groups, and another minister, an intergroup council was formed, and the desegregation issue was taken to City Hall and, finally, to the local Federal Housing Office. At long last the white housing project became integrated, and many of the families in our area who had waited so long to leave the rats, the broken stairs, the stink, and the uncollected garbage moved in. But again, the ways of the world intervened. The housing project went a complete circle from all white to racial balance to all black within a few years. "Now that it's just us again, they'll be calling this a slum," said Mrs. Smith, Dennis's mother and one of its first Negro tenants.

We finally grew accustomed to the snail's pace of reform and the terrible difficulty the poor encountered in performing what we used to think were the simplest of everyday tasks. To pay a bill meant taking the cash (and often standing in line for a money order, too) in order to wait for the bus in order to meet the creditor. A sick child did not involve calling the doctor from the phone in the kitchen and picking up the prescription at the drugstore. It meant going to the phone booth to call Emergency and waiting for the ambulance, or taking the bus to sit in the outpatient clinic to wait for the interns, and finally to be confronted with the bill again. Sheer, massive torpor was the result. Why bother to come on time or even to come to the meeting, the school, the church? Far easier to say, "I couldn't make it."

XIX *Farewell*

When our eighth year began, we didn't know that it would be our last. Paul had had bouts of undefined infections, to which the doctor had given the all-inclusive label of "cumulative fatigue." Harry said it was a pretty long way of saying Poppy was tired out. There were other considerations in addition to health. Marian, our baby, was almost one; Honor, our eldest, was eleven. We were expecting our seventh child in early summer. The rectory was crowded; we needed more room and time for family life. Everything had piled up. We were ready to go.

Before Christmas, 1956, Paul went with our elder children to Fort Dix to pick up a Hungarian couple whom we had sponsored, refugees from the revolution that had just taken place. Our children remember the outline of the Statue of Liberty against the sky as they drove over the Jersey flats, and the endless papers that had to be signed, sorted, or found at the refugee center before the tired couple was released. That first night, Trudy, pink-cheeked and eight months pregnant, described for us the anguish of crossing icy fields and barbed-wire fences to the Andau bridge as she and her husband Janos escaped into Austria. The next day she complained about the Jersey City beauty parlor where her blond hair had been washed because the proprietor was a Jew. She and her husband spent Christmas with us and brought us Hungarian chocolates they had smuggled out in Janos's knapsack. We drank wine in honor of the occasion. But before the holiday dinner was over, there was a call from the police, followed quickly by one from Naomi. James had been shot in the stomach by the owner of a shop he had tried to rob on Christmas afternoon. He had broken the plate-glass window, thinking no one would be there that day, and was shot by the proprietor. He was still holding the crumpled six dollars, all he had found in the cash drawer, when the police arrived.

By Christmas night the bullet was removed, and Paul called from the hospital to tell us James was resting comfortably and would be well. (Later, James served a jail sentence.) It was our last Jersey City Christmas.

Death had claimed many of our early intimates. Mrs. Raymond, across the backyard, had died two years before. When we first knew her, she had said over and over that she hoped she'd mend enough to come back to church someday. She never came. She looked out the window and twirled the radio dial with her stiffening fingers. All we could do for her was wave, bring our children to see her, assure her that Jerome was a fine man, and bury her from the church whose tower she had watched in the changing sky. When she died, a neighbor who kept an extra door key for Jerome rushed over to tell us. The neighbor had been concerned when she hadn't heard the familiar radio and had let herself in. When she saw the slumped figure in the arm chair and heard the cat moving, she knew right off. Then she ran to us. She and I helped Paul carry Mrs. Raymond from the chair to the bed. The cat followed in our footsteps, and suddenly the old body seemed small and as lonely as the milk bottle washed and shiny outside the door. Jerome never said much about any of it except to comment that she must have died minutes after he went to work, or else the radio would have been on full blast. He wore his blue suit at the funeral, and afterwards he went off to live in the suburbs with his married sister. His mother's landlord bought up the furniture and rented the three rooms to a Puerto Rican family. There were already Puerto Ricans upstairs.

Once in a while Jerome came to see us. "That commute's no good," he told us. He traveled thirty miles each day from East Orange to the Jersey Central train yards. "Cleaning coaches ain't what it used to be. Some's as old as I am." He looked back across the yard at his mother's window, flower pots crowding the sill where the cat used to be.

"There wasn't a spik here till five years ago," he said, shaking his head.

George, the bum with the El Greco face, had died. Harry brought us the news. "He must have got up from the doorway where he was sleepin' and hit his head against the curb when he fell. I was comin' from the public bath when the cops found him, but I stuck close to the walls—scared they'd pick me up as accessory to the watcha-call-it."

Harry had gathered together the men who congregated at our door for coffee and grandly announced the hour of George's funeral. About six of the regulars came, including garrulous Clarence, strangely silent in red-faced sobriety for his friend's service. Those who were in shirt sleeves came to the house beforehand to get jackets from our basement old-clothes room. Their faces, lined from drink and doorway nights, had an embarrassed look as they faced the responsibility of being present at an event. They sat in their second-hand suits in the front of the church, the smell of old alcohol breath mixing with the lemon fragrance of the wooden pews. Harry and Horace served as pallbearers—Harry, stiff and formal in his rented Marine blues, Horace little boy-like in his confusion as to how he should react to death. Neither of them had let the casket on its carriage move more than a foot away from them. What money we could gather went for the casket, and George was buried in a pauper's grave.

In 1957 peoples' pocketbooks were fuller than they had been in 1949. Lucille's three little boys were in school, but she still sat out front with a new baby girl in the carriage. Her husband's job in a munitions factory gave them more money to spend, and occasionally the whole family went to a lake for the day in their car. There was more prosperity after the Korean war—or, more properly, less destitution. There were television sets, some telephones, a few cars where there had been none of these things, and some public housing that was better, at least in the beginning, than the rat-ridden alley tenements.

The sea captain was older, but it was not so much his age as our own familiarity with his scowl and the crippled foot that always stuck out in front of him that made him seem milder to us now. Howdy still sold lemon ice and other confections; our children, holding Rosie by the hand, walked around the corner almost every afternoon to spend their nickels. Even he seemed softer, and when I went for the evening paper, he acknowledged my appearance by tossing the *Jersey Journal* over the counter without waiting for me to ask. Sometimes when I had our two-year-old George along, he would poke the boy's pink cheeks and say, "Cute one, that."

Many of the activities had been transferred from the rectory to space in the building down the street; part of the staff lived there, too. A volunteer from the early years came back to visit and told us how stuffy and conservative we had become now that the rectory traffic had subsided. But as he teased me, a Puerto Rican in a sombrero climbed through our open living room window, did a silent soft-shoe routine in front of the sofa where the volunteer sat, and retired just as soundlessly through the window at the other end of the room.

The neighborhood had changed in eight years. Puerto Ricans were moving in, and a Spanish club and Spanish service had been added to the Grace Church program. Negroes were living nearer the church, in what had once been a white area.

Finally we were about to leave. There were others, younger and stronger, to take our place. Paul was to announce our departure for a downtown church in Indianapolis. He had been offered the job in late spring, and we had decided almost immediately to accept. He lunched with Charles Beckwith, the lawyer, his closest friend in Jersey City, to tell him in confidence ahead of time of our move. Charles seemed to understand. Early that Sunday, the day of the announcement, Charles came to the rectory door and asked for me. He stood with his hat in his hand, turning the brim around in his fingers, and spoke with a one-sided smile on his face. "You're going because you don't like us after all, isn't that it?"

I tried to argue, but the tears came too fast and too hard, and I ran upstairs. Paul found me and kissed me, and then I walked around the block and stumbled by people I knew.

From the pulpit, Paul told everyone that we were leaving and what the years had meant. There were a few long pauses, but he managed. People thanked us, congratulated us ("It must be a promotion"). They said they'd miss us. Somehow we got through it all—the tears, the good-byes, the presents, the testimonial dinner, the speeches. Even Cousin Helen sent a telegram. Charles and I never talked about my tearful outburst in the front hall.

When the moving van came, Dennis and his brother Sammy hung around until late at night, when it was finally loaded and locked. In the morning, there was endless standing on the street while the truck was checked again and rumbled off. The Coreys came, Mae stamping out lipsticked cigarettes on the curb and talking about the old days. Horace, with Mary's little girl (Mary was working at the dime store, he told us), was there until the very end. Harry took the departure as a personal insult and swore at us as we said goodbye. Lucille kissed me and went back to her stoop to wave.

I don't remember driving away.

Epilogue

Six or seven years ago, I returned to Second Street. It was easier than the first few visits when memories were fresh. Faces on the block were still familiar. Mothers waved, shook my hand, embraced me, asked for the children and the priests. Where were they all now, they wanted to know. And Father Moore's job in Indiana—a more successful church, more space for the kids to play? I smiled; a word or two was answer enough.

Theirs was the same, familiar refrain: "Things are changing here." Two houses on the block had gone colored, they said. Lucille, blond as ever, had moved. She and her husband were managing a motel near a New Jersey lake; their kids were attending a brand-new school. The Polish sea captain and Mr. D'Agostino had died a week apart around Christmas. Mr. D'Agostino, with no known relatives and his business bankrupt, was buried in a pauper's grave. Boards had been nailed over the broken windows (vandals, they explained) of his vacant undertaking establishment. Some of the Negro tenements, including Dennis's old building, had been torn down two years before. There was talk of new low-cost housing, but it was only a promise, the women said, like everything else. There was a new supermarket around the corner, though, and two four-story apartment buildings that were supposed to attract middle-income people to the neighborhood.

Conversation petered out. I said I'd be back to visit again next year, and continued down the block toward Howdy's store. I was bursting with excitement at seeing it again. (I had not been there since we left.) *My* neighborhood, *my* candy store where my children had spent eight years' worth of allowances—surely, I thought, Howdy and I will be able to reminisce.

A little girl was standing with her nose pressed against the glass of the candy bins. Howdy sat on his high stool behind the counter, picking his teeth and reading the funny papers.

"Remember me?" I asked brightly.

He stopped picking his teeth to grunt wordlessly at my outstretched hand. A shiny cash register had replaced the drawer in which he had surreptitiously collected money in earlier years. "Things are getting a lot fancier around here," I ventured, pointing at the new object.

"The niggers held up my store," he answered, standing to tip a scoopful of jelly beans into a paper bag for the little girl, who laboriously extracted some pennies from the pocket of her cotton dress and let them clatter from her fingers to the counter top. "Take all day, will you, kid?" Howdy pushed the coins with the side of one hand, collected them in the other, counted them out loud, and dropped them in the register.

"I heard you moved," he said, looking at me finally.

"It's more than three years now," I answered. He had already turned to wait on a new customer. Hoping to feel less idiotic, I waved good-bye, but his head was bent over the whirring blade of his slicing machine, a hunk of salami in his left hand, and he didn't notice. I was crushed. But Howdy was right—we had moved from Second Street.

Soon after we arrived in Indianapolis, a milkman came to

bid for our voluminous order. "What beautiful blue eyes you have," he said to five-year-old Rosie. "Our whole family does," she replied, and for me the years in Indianapolis were, for the most part, years with the "whole family." Two more babies were born, but despite all the children our new life seemed almost dull after the excitement of the rectory in Jersey City. It was a less earthy existence, but the change was deeper than that. What we had not fully realized when we arrived in Indianapolis in the fall of 1957 was the deep change that had taken place in us during our eight years in Jersey City. We were never able to put into words how much we had become a part of Second Street and how much Second Street had become a part of us. The assumptions and fears of comfortable, white America, with which we were once again surrounded after having been away so long, wounded us. Second Street had protected us, and we were suddenly very vulnerable. We felt guilty that we had left.

At first, I didn't know what to do with myself. The rectory that came with Paul's job as Dean of the Cathedral was huge and was directly across the street from the house where, it was said, the John Birch Society had first met. Our house had wall-to-wall carpeting, two wall ovens, a laundry chute. Clotheslines flapping in the Jersey City sky were only a memory. The rectory was fifteen minutes away from the church downtown, and Paul commuted to work like anybody else. People came to his office with their problems, instead of to our kitchen. There was no longer the likelihood of suddenly finding a family huddled on our doorstep after having been evicted—a commonplace so recently. Where before we had confronted directly the elemental needs of shelter, food, and clothing, and dealt with them on our doorstep or in our house, Paul now went through "channels." The results were good but the approach was different, and for a long time we felt ourselves in no-man's land.

Much of Paul's time in Indianapolis was devoted to getting a middle-class congregation actively involved in the problems of the rest of the city. The response was often warm and willing; the process was generally slow and painful, for the more "powerful" is the church in the community, the more it is involved in the status quo and the less likely it is to speak out on social injustice. During our six years there, I was involved in school integration committees and the Fair Housing Association (our Indianapolis neighborhood was also "changing"). We were happy there. It was a wrench to leave.

Since January, 1964, Paul has been Suffragan (that is assistant) Bishop of Washington, (D.C.), and has had to deal with yet another aspect of the same problems in yet another city. We live in a brick house on a shady, tree-lined street among government people, journalists, politicians, among many who are deeply concerned about the Second Streets of Washington and elsewhere. Honor, our eldest, fulfilling her role as doll-parade manager in front of Grace Church Rectory, is in her first year at the Yale School of Drama, specializing in production. Pip, now called Paul, is a Yale junior, writing for the college newspaper and majoring in political science. Dee is a freshman at Radcliffe, having spent her high school years organizing students from all over the city to push for better public education in the District of Columbia. The other six children attend Washington public schools.

Kim recently succeeded Bishop Pike as Bishop of California, and Bob is in a parish in Maryland. Both of them married and have families. Bishop Washburn retired almost ten years ago and died in 1966.

And what of Jersey City? It was a city of 300,000 when we lived there, somewhat larger than it is today. Now there are more Negroes, fewer whites, and the Puerto Rican population—only hundreds in the early fifties—is counted in the thousands. Ecumenism, as remote as the Garden of Eden when we lived in the shadow of St. Mary's Roman Catholic Church, is now a fact of everyday life. Barriers are down between our sisters and the Roman Catholic nuns. Clergy of all denominations are joining together for social action where formerly Protestants had cooperated only on a committee level and there had been no relationship at all with Roman Catholics.

Boys we knew are employed as leaders in the local Jersey poverty programs. Some are in jail for murder, some push dope; a few are Black Muslims; a number are teachers, union officials, school principals, settlement house workers; some are in Viet Nam. Girls have been married and divorced, some only once, others over and over; some are still content with the boy they kissed on our doorstep; others have seven or eight children and are still unmarried. Some died young of tuberculosis or in childbirth, and one of Dennis's brothers died in an apartment fire. Naomi's retarded brother, now in his late teens, was finally accepted in an institution. Louise died of alcoholism in her twenties—she went very fast, they say. There seems to be no trace of the Coreys, Mae, Frank, or children. Dennis, married and a father, has a steady job in a factory. Mrs. Hyde's son is an artist, but he works in a New York City post office. Her daughter teaches English at City College in the Bronx. Naomi and James still live with their one child in Naomi's mother's apartment, the one that was the prize for voting "right." James is employed at General Electric and works actively in the Grace Church recreation program with a new generation of boys. Some of the older generation are the church's leaders. Many of their children play in the front yard of the rectory and bounce balls against the wall next door, although in general the atmosphere seems more sedate than in our time.

Diocesan support of a team ministry continued into the 1960's under Bishop Washburn's successor. Recently there has been a cutback in funds and the parish has been encouraged to become self-supporting. As a result there is but one priest in the rectory now. He is loving and hard-working, but handicapped by having staff help only in the summers and on weekends. The narrow wooden rectory stairs have been carpeted in dark red by a devoted church member. I found myself wondering how Mrs. Powell would react to the carpet when I walked on its soft pile on a recent visit.

But there is more to Second Street than stair carpeting and vital statistics about our friends, more to our eight years there than nostalgia. Jersey City changed our lives, but how did we change our small part of Jersey City? What did we accomplish? What can be accomplished in a time of riots and calls for black separatism?

No one has to tell us that we didn't begin to change the system except to smooth some of its edges, and those impermanently. Although today there are more jobs available, more public housing, more telephones, cars, and better plumbing, the hard, cold, unassailable fact remains that the people on Second Street live outside that world that grows more affluent with every turn. They are still politically powerless, groggy from television's half-truths, patronized by handouts from a grossly inefficient welfare system. We changed none of that. But we did live there as a family; we were part of the community; we had no contract to fulfill. We didn't sign up for two years to work a block, and when there were parish projects we didn't calculate the amount of "feasible participation of the poor." We were never that efficient, and our criteria for evaluating our work were as vague as the facts of Harry's circus career.

We were neither a family guidance service nor social workers, although Bob, Kim, and Paul had had some counseling training in seminary. In an age of growing super-specialization, we were untutored generalists. Perhaps it would have been professional to give Mrs. Powell some ideas for a balanced diet realistic for her tiny pension, had I had that kind of knowledge. But we liked Mrs. Powell, and we laughed with her. She was fun, and I have a feeling that it was her own sense of worth as a person, which our mutual enjoyment of one another helped keep alive, that sustained her. I know any grocery list I might have given her would have shot its way over the table (holding her Manhattan cocktail) in a rapidly constructed spitball. It might have been helpful to George, the El Greco bum, if we could have taught him to cane chairs, but I haven't a shadow of a doubt that it was more important that he had a home to visit on Second Street where no demands would be made, where no one would try to "improve" him. It could have proved constructive if we'd had more psychiatric help for many of the children who came around; it would certainly have been a help to have had more than one remedial reading teacher.

All those things might have improved the lot of our Jersey City friends, but they were not as important as our simply being *there*. Primarily—and leaving aside psychological motives from our own backgrounds—we lived on Second Street because we believed in God and in the unique worth of every person. The concept sometimes seemed either too simple or too complex—I've never known which—for daily certitude (there *were* mornings when we would wake up and wonder what we were doing there). Nonetheless, it overarched our lives like the Jersey City clotheslines. I believe it worked. I know that the boys who played ball in our yard and grew into the men who hate "Whitey" today remember the talks when they were in their teens around our kitchen table: about girls and sex, about being black, about Africa, about Jersey City politics. Even though they may hate "Whitey" now, I persist that to a man they could walk this moment into our house on the shady, tree-lined street in Washington and there would still be no barriers between us. And breaking down barriers is what I have been talking about.

In the summer of 1964, Paul returned from three weeks in Mississippi. I met him in the airport at Newark, where we read in the evening paper of a riot under way, presumably at that very moment, in our old area of Jersey City. We changed our plans about returning to Washington and drove over to the rectory. We joined the people sitting, as always, in the kitchen, and learned that the violence had started when a woman was arrested. Someone had jumped on the hood of a police car, threats were exchanged, windows and windshields broken. The telephone rang with rumors of further violence. James came by and Paul drove with him to join the Grace Church clergy nearer the trouble. There, Paul kept meeting old friends, young men whom he had known as boys. They embraced him with the arms that didn't hold the Molotov cocktails. Soon after he arrived, police opened fire in earnest. He and an old Grace Church boy fled from the gunfire while mounted police charged in formation down the middle of the street. Paul and others pleaded with the police to cordon off the whole section. No one really seemed to know what was happening. There was fear and ignorance on the part of some policemen, who took no apparent action to conciliate grievances or to isolate the actual violence. Even a visit to City Hall that evening showed a complete lack of understanding when boys who volunteered to cool down the crowd were turned away. By midnight, all that was left was broken glass, a few people hurt, confusion, and anger on both sides. Obviously, Paul was no white Malcolm X who could have succeeded in controlling the crowd with a word, nor were his successors at Grace Church who were closer to the immediate situation. But he was still a friend after seven years and, even under gunfire, the Jersey City men he knew didn't forget it.

So to the Watts, the Detroits, the Newarks of the long, hot summers, to the frightening assumption that other equally violent summers will follow, that winters may get to be like summers—does any of this point to an answer? I believe that it does—tentative, embryonic perhaps, but nonetheless valid. Friendship is such a fragile thing and barriers seem so much easier to throw up than to break down that establishing a connection with another human being is a tenuous business at best. Yet once established, it is more enduring in many ways than massively financed official programs. No one makes friends with a program; it takes a person and the person must be there for a long time, living in the slums and the ghettos. I can give no guidelines for the living of such lives today in this other America. I only know it must still be done.

A few months ago, a boy whom we knew well in Jersey City visited us in Washington. He used to come to all the dances, he played ball in the rectory yard, he sat and talked in our kitchen. I remembered him from Christmases, from hot summers, from scrawled letters ("Dear Friends, I like this fresh air camp"), from seeing him shine shoes in the subway at rush hour. I remembered his telephoning from the bar at the corner that his father was drunk and beating up his mother, and would one of the priests come over. He was like hundreds of other boys we knew. The children were out playing and Paul was not at home when he arrived at our house in Washington, so he and I talked the whole long afternoon. He had finished two years at a Negro college down South on an athletic scholarship. Twenty-seven, married, and the father of two, he was holding down two jobs. He still lived in Jersey City. We talked of all the friends we both remembered, of their lives, the poverty, the rats, the housing, of his father's drinking, of how it has felt to be a Negro over the years since we had known each other so well.

"Before you came," he said to me finally, "we had very little hope, but you started a chain of things. There was camp and different experiences like that, and when there was nothing else to do we could go to Grace Church and hang around.

You were the first white people we didn't hate. There was love and care for a long time."

I must have looked startled, because he touched my arm as we sat on the sofa and went on to explain, "You're too hard on yourself. You mean you didn't know people remembered the love? Anyone could tell you. Even the guys who don't give a damn about God will admit that when you pin them down."

Washington, D.C.
December, 1967